HIGH ON THE CAMPUS

HIGH ON THE CAMPUS

student drug abuse
is there an answer?

gordon r. mc lean
haskell bowen

2011

Tyndale House Publishers
Wheaton, Illinois

Coverdale House Publishers Ltd.
London and Eastbourne, England

Distributed in Canada by
Home Evangel Books Ltd.
Toronto, Ontario

Library of Congress Catalog Number 75-123031
SBN No. 8423-1430-X, cloth
SBN No. 8423-1431-8, paper

Copyright © 1970 by Tyndale House Publishers,
Wheaton, Illinois.

Printed in U. S. A.

Dedicated to

Mr. Robert Nino
Chief Probation Officer
Juvenile Court
Santa Clara County, California

. . . a man whose wisdom and concern has
built one of the best juvenile programs in
the nation.

CONTENTS

A WORD FROM THE AUTHORS

We wish to express our deep appreciation to the various educational, law enforcement, and youth organizations as well as the various authors and publications quoted in this book—all of these people have given us valuable assistance.

We wish to especially thank:

The judges and staff of the Santa Clara County Juvenile Court as well as the young men at the county juvenile rehabilitation facilities. The boys helped us greatly with suggestions, their own experiences, and contributed the very interesting list of drug abuse terms at the end of the book.

Lieutenant Stanley Hardman and the narcotics unit of the San Jose Police Department.

Dr. Glenn Hoffman, Superintendent of the Santa Clara County Schools; Dr. Nicholas Montesano, superintendent, the principals and staff of the Campbell Union High School District, with whom the authors have worked closely.

Business leaders in the community who have lent valuable assistance in building our drug abuse program, including Conn Bauer, Glen George, Dick Norman, and Ed Stirm.

The Board of Directors of Drug Abuse Information Service and Santa Clara Valley Youth for Christ/Campus Life, and the staff in YFC Campus Life across the nation, as well as the director of our local high school program, Jim Buchfuehrer.

We appreciate the assistance of the various authors and publishers who have allowed us to use their material as background or quote from their sources:

Ann Landers of the *Chicago Sun-Times* and Publishers - Hall Syndicate.

Harold Myra, Dean Merrill, and the staff of *Campus Life* magazine, a publication of Youth for Christ International.

The editors of *Focus on Youth,* a publication of Young Life, and the editors of *Listen* magazine.

Harper & Rowe, Publishers, for quotes from Dr. William Glasser's book, *Schools Without Failure.*

McGraw-Hill Publishing Company for quotes from *The Drug Scene* by Dr. Donald B. Louria.

Simon and Schuster, Inc., for quotes from *The Birth of God* by James Kavanaugh, published in 1969 by Trident Press.

John Wiley and Sons, Inc. for a quote from *Law Enforcement and the Youthful Offender* by Edward Eldefonso.

The editors of *The Christian Science Monitor, Newsweek, Time* and *Life* for background material.

Harold Streeter of the *San Francisco Examiner*

and Sam Hanson, education editor of the *San Jose Mercury,* for use of their material on our drug abuse assembly programs in the schools.

The *San Jose News* and *Campus Life* magazine for photos.

The title for the book was suggested by Art Blodgett, for two years student body president of Mount Pleasant High School, San Jose.

We are grateful to the various sources quoted and to official agencies who cooperated with us in the preparation of this material, but the authors alone are responsible for the views expressed on these pages.

Finally, we wish to thank Mr. Art Linkletter and Mr. C. M. Vandeburg for their invaluable counsel, assistance, and for the introduction for this book, as well as our young friend Pat for his foreword.

Gordon McLean and Haskell Bowen

INTRODUCTION

I know from bitter, tragic experience that parents are too often apt to underrate the drug abuse problem in America today.

All of us are prone to believe that it can't happen here. We think that drugs are an evil that plagues only the ignorant, the stranger, or the underprivileged.

I have learned firsthand that the extent of the drug craze is unbelievable! Its projected increase is frightening. Its penetration into all classes, all levels of society, all ages of school children, and all neighborhoods is fantastic.

No one segment of our society can cope with this chemical forest fire that is consuming not only our young people, but middle-class adults as well.

Parents must become knowledgeable. Educators must become responsibly aware. The government must reevaluate its role and sponsor better laws and more understanding law enforcement, in light of modern thinking and the latest scientific research.

And finally, the young people themselves must be motivated with the truth. Nothing else will be truly effective, I believe, until the kids make up their minds that drug taking is "out."

The moment that most of our young people decide that it's stupid and wasteful to "turn on, tune in, and drop out," the drug abuse problem will be on the way to solution.

This book should help parents, teachers, and youngsters to know "where it's at!" Stripped of mythology, panic reaction, and trite moralisms, it presents a clear summary of the problem and its ramifications, and suggests what can best be done on the basis of many attempts by communities across the nation. The "case histories" should be read by every responsible person concerned with this problem.

I wish I had been able to read it before we lost our lovely Diane.

Art Linkletter

FOREWORD

I was in court for furnishing drugs. You might not think so to meet me. My hair is not long, I dress conservatively, and I hold no way-out philosophies. From all outward appearances, I'm just a typical high school student.

But I got introduced to the drug scene early in my high school days, starting out with a few joints and going on to try a number of other drugs. Furnishing was an easy step from there.

The tragedy of drugs has affected my family as well. My sister's husband, with whom I was involved, was a heavy dealer and brought my sister into his activities. Another brother-in-law has been strung out for a long time while his younger brother, age sixteen, was at the county juvenile rehabilitation ranch because of his steady use of speed. I'm hoping he can be helped off drugs and stay clean, but it will be a long, hard battle.

There is much ignorance about drugs. As a result a lot of wild statements are made, and scare tactics are used. It doesn't work. Any material not honestly presented to us fails. Once adults exaggerate, they lose us.

Most parents really know very little about drugs and tend to either panic or ignore the problem hoping it will go away. It isn't apt to. They tend to learn from other parents—not all of whom are really well-informed. I love my parents a great deal, but they were not equipped to cope with what was happening in our family. My drug involvement wasn't stopped until I was busted and shortly thereafter met Mr. McLean and Mr. Bowen, authors of this book.

I went to court facing the possibility of confinement in a juvenile institution or transfer to adult court from which I might be sent to the county jail farm. While awaiting my hearing, I wrote a letter to the judge who would decide my case. I meant every word I put down. Here is a part of that letter:

"I have found out, Sir, that a person cannot build a life of pretending because that life is being built on false pretenses.

"The ten days I spent at your facilities were the most worthwhile ten days I had ever had. It seems hard to believe because they were also the most agonizing and painful days, not only for me, but for my parents who were really hurt because I was in trouble. I am thankful I was locked up for a couple of reasons. First, I was given time to really examine my life and my attitude and to determine which direction I was going. Second, I had time to think about the rotten crowd I'd been seeing for two miserable years. The result: a decision to stay away from them!

"As you probably already know, Your Honor, I have been deeply involved in the drug scene. When I first started to accept the drug way of life, my personality made a change—a change that made me close my eyes to the fact I was doing wrong. Instead of expressing the idea that bad was bad, I was turning bad into something good and enjoyable which became a part of my life. I must say the greater part of my life, because it was eventually taking over. As that happened I lost interest in studies and my good activities.

"My first meeting with the police was six months ago. I was charged with being in a car where the driver had dangerous drugs and marijuana. When I was in juvenile hall for two and a half days, nobody really showed me the seriousness of my crime, and I didn't realize it myself. Of course nobody but me could make me change. I didn't learn anything, and was released on an informal supervision.

"The situation is now different—and so am I. I do know this—because of what I have decided and with God's help—I will never use drugs again. I can and will end my problems in juvenile court, which is where I hope my case will be handled. My parents want and need me at home—my dad has been ill— but I'll be of help to them only if I'm doing the right thing, and this I plan to do.

"I want to finish my senior year in high school, which should go much better with my mind un-clogged from drugs. While doing this, I will continue to share some of my experiences with high school kids, helping Mr. McLean and Mr. Bowen in their drug abuse programs, and I think kids will listen to someone their own age telling them what can happen. I've already done several of these programs, trying to be part of the solution instead of the problem. I also intend to work with the Campus Life Clubs, trying to reach kids before they meet the tragedy that I have been living with for the past two years.

"I wrote you because you may have people in your court every day saying they'll quit doing wrong, and then they're back again in more trouble later. That could make you very disappointed. But I also hope you've had many who have made good. And no matter what happens, I intend to make good."

The judge read my letter and heard the other evidence, and he believed me. I was kept in juvenile court and released home on probation, which is admittedly a very lenient disposition.

I've been busy since then keeping my word and making sure the leniency shown was not wasted. I've talked with hundreds of young people about the drug problem, and we've had some great sessions. I think we're getting across to many of them.

Now, through this book, Mr. McLean, Mr. Bowen, Mr. Linkletter, and I want to reach out to parents and students alike.

For me, this book is important. If someone had placed something like this in my hands two years ago, I might never have been involved with drugs. Perhaps you and your family will be more fortunate than we were. I hope so.

—Pat M.

THE TURNED ON GENERATION AND THEIR PARENTS

38 STUDENTS HELD IN DRUG SALE ROUNDUP screamed the headlines in the morning paper. The story underneath gave details of an extensive police investigation, conducted over several months, resulting in the arrest of the suspects charged with furnishing marijuana, seconal, LSD, methedrine, and benzedrine. Many of those arrested were juniors and seniors in high school. All of them came from the better and more affluent sections of the community.

Stories like this no longer are unusual in many cities across the nation. California alone experienced a 2,000 percent increase in juvenile drug arrests over a six-year period, the state attorney-general recently reported. It is estimated that from 20 to 30 percent of the students in high school have experimented with drugs in some form. For every juvenile arrested, it is safe to estimate there are thirty to fifty who do not come to the attention of authorities. Los Angeles officials estimate $250,000 is spent every day on illegal drugs in their city alone.

1

San Francisco spends $3.75 million annually for the hospital care required by approximately five thousand teen-age drug users. New York City recently reported its youngest drug death—an eleven-year-old boy who had taken an overdose of heroin. Dr. Hardin B. Jones of the University of California at Berkeley comments that "drug abuse, which moved from the slums to our college campuses, has now infected the entire spectrum of our schools and is spilling over into the middle-class adult world as well. The extent of this drug craze is unbelievable and its projected increase is frightening."

Parents, particularly, are concerned, anxious, and just plain scared. For most students, the use of drugs is a once-in-awhile event. For others, it has become a way of life perhaps because the experimenting can't, at least for them, be limited. These young people happen to be susceptible to certain drugs, become dependent, and get badly hurt from what may have started out as an innocent adventure.

Complicating the problem is the fact that we live in a drug-oriented society. We produce new alcoholics in this nation at the rate of fifty an hour. And millions of people are addicted to cigarettes, though they usually insist they can quit anytime. "It's easy, I've done it hundreds of times!" they say.

Truck drivers and students cramming for a test often will take pep pills to keep them awake, or persuade a doctor to give them diet pills to lose weight. Dangerous? Ask Dr. David Smith of the University of California Medical Center and the Haight-Ashbury Medical Clinic in San Francisco.

"If the habit grows, they move into the pill stage

and start buying pills on the black market," Smith says. "Amphetamines stimulate the nervous system, which means the 'high' is followed by depression. Then the individual treats his depression by going back up again. The prolonged use of 'speed' or other amphetamines produces severe psychiatric problems, visual and auditory hallucinations, and paranoia. Actually, the major drug problem in the Haight-Ashbury district was the use of amphetamines. Large numbers of young people taking amphetamines interacted in a violent and hostile way. Amphetamines seem to be the only drugs in which we find a direct correlation to violence."

For a growing number of adults, drugs are a way of life. They take pep pills to get up, tranquilizers to stay calm, a cocktail to start the evening, and a barbiturate to go to sleep. It can make for a very short day of rational thinking.

The young are also influenced by a growing number of movies and songs glorifying the use of drugs. There is nothing secretive about it. Through their music and in pictures, the cool generation is telling the squares what is happening. We agree the use of drug terms popular in modern speech doesn't mean young people are going to be influenced to take drugs, any more than the use of the phrase "This is murder!" means you're going to commit one. But the trend towards drug promotion and vulgarity in music is not a healthy one—dirty words used to be scrawled on walls; now they're flashed on screens or on "top 40" records.

In these pages we'll be taking a look at various aspects of the drug problem, including the drugs young people use and their effects. But perhaps we should begin with the all-important question, "Why?" Jim Smith and the editors of *Campus Life* magazine analyzed various student surveys and came out with eight reasons for student drug involvement.

"Man, there is just nothing else to do!" Caught in the monotony of living (one day like the next like the next like the next), a wild trip on drugs offers forbidden excitement. Most would think our modern, fast-paced society leaves little room for boredom. But one student expressed it this way: "The world seems dull lots of times—we're over-titillated." Which means that there's too much outside stimulation. As Dr. Keniston of Yale explains: "A person can become psychologically numb, overwhelmed by all the stimuli and pressures around him, the demands for his attention. He puts up a screen to ignore it all. But this self-erected screen may become so dense it isolates him from direct experience with the simple, the beautiful, and the unexpected in the world around him."

Without a healthy interest in the little things around him, and bored by routine, this student finds that moments of exhilaration and danger give life zest—for a little while.

"I lose all my worries and imagine many things." To the student who worries about the future, about grades, about what people are thinking or saying about him or her, drugs become a reassuring lollipop to suck on, a security blanket to curl up with. Retreat via drugs from the harsh—or imagined harsh—realities of life drives the user even further away.

"It blows my parents' minds. They just can't

believe their little girl is on pot!" This is one way students hit back at parents—to shock them, loosen them up a bit. Taking drugs is an outward rejection of society in general. One psychiatrist says, "It is fun for them to see their parents get put on. Drugs give them something with which to get their parents enraged and incensed."

"I just can't take all the tension." The gigantic pressure cooker most high schoolers are in—the cooker which demands high grades, heavy participation, and being a social swinger—proves too much for some. It's especially tough when a student tries like crazy yet ends up with C's, and it doesn't look as though he'll make that prestige college—or when his frazzled nerves tell him he's taken on too much, but he doesn't see any way out.

Dr. William Glasser discusses some of these issues in his controversial and provocative book on contemporary American education, *Schools without Failure.*

The goals of education as Dr. Glasser sees them are: ". . . to give people the mental tools to deal effectively with new situations, to place fewer restrictions on their lives caused by fear of difficult problems, and to enable people to deal with new situations and difficult problems rationally rather than emotionally."

He sees some definite limitation in reaching these goals that, among other things, are very frustrating to the students: "As long as we look upon students as empty vessels to be filled with facts, as long as we train them to be computers to give us predictable answers to predictable questions, we are building into the most basic institution of democracy, the educational system, the seeds of its own destruction."

Further, "The children realize that they have no part in making decisions about their behavior or their participation in school. Taught formally from kindergarten about the value of our democratic way of life, children learn from experience that the major premise of a democratic society—that the people involved in any endeavor help determine its rules—does not apply to them."

What of the classrooms and subject material? Glasser comments, "Too much school material is unrealistic, unemotional and dull. . . . A totally quiet, orderly, unemotional class is rarely learning. . . . Grades have become a substitute for learning, the symbolic replacement of knowledge. One's transcript is more important than one's knowledge. The colleges of America which admit primarily on the basis of high grades are major culprits in an unpremeditated plot to destroy the students. . . . When grades become the substitute for learning, and when they become more important than what is learned, they tend to lower academic standards." Another destructive and frustrating practice in the school system Dr. Glasser attacks is the "assignment of excessive, tedious, and often irrelevant homework."

"Me? I was just curious, that's all." Dr. Mitchell Balter found in his survey of teens that about a third who experiment with drugs do so out of curiosity. With all the talk going on about Yellow Jackets, Double Trouble, Giggle Smoke, Speedballs, and Speed, even though the dangers are clearly pointed

out, the desire to "try some and see" becomes tragically strong for some otherwise levelheaded kids. Educational programs, poorly presented, sometimes add to this problem. One student commented, "If drugs were worth canceling classes to talk about, they were worth trying!"

"I don't mind saying it. I'm just a failure, that's all." If you could look deep into the thoughts and feelings of many students, you'd find they considered themselves "nothing much," and that their clumsiness or their being overweight or their low grades or their rejection by other students keeps them from feeling self-assured. They may quickly cluster with other students who don't feel they're making it either—but they all can get some "high and good" feelings through drugs.

"Drugs will help me realize my true potential." We are bombarded every day by more sense impressions than we can absorb. What is required is skill to choose what has or has not relevance to our particular goal. But the hostile, the confused, and the inept seek instant transformation by way of drugs. All that is needed, they believe, is to swallow the magic potion and their true value will be revealed to a humbled world. So the alchemists dreamed of an elixir to make them wise; so bottled sunshine was peddled from the tailgates of medicine-show wagons.

"Drugs will help me find a new religious experience and forget myself." The goal of true religion is *not* to forget yourself. It is discipline of self. This is not the same as slopping through the cosmos with no identity. The Christian injunction is to lose one's

life in order to find it. The stress is on the acquisition of authentic identity, a self. The emphasis is on "mind," "attention," "find." These the drug advocates shrug off in favor of "no mind," "relax," "lose." Anybody can do that: it's easy. Exactly.

Alienation from the adult society is one of the strongest factors in creating the insecurity for which drugs have become a way out, and it is a reason parents, teachers, and the community establishment have the hardest time understanding. In this alienation is wrapped up all the campus unrest, the so-called generation gap, and the problem of drug abuse.

And the problem begins at home. Many young people involved with drugs come from what appear to be normal homes, but just beneath the surface of modern, suburban, split-level tract living often may be found emotional unbalance. Families are striving so hard for success that they give their children things instead of guidance and love. Alcoholism and unhappy marriage relationships frequently end in separation and divorce.

Parents often are afraid of their teen-agers, so no limits or disciplinary standards are set. "They all let their kids . . ." becomes a guideline for weak-willed parents and a rallying-point for overbearing adolescents. Parents encourage sexual promiscuity, use of alcohol or drugs, and other problems by leaving children too much on their own with no supervision or even knowledge of their whereabouts. Unlimited access to the automobile is another strong factor in molding teen-age standards. For the more responsible, a car can be a step toward adult living; for the immature, it can be a ticket to disaster.

In other homes, an exaggerated sense of authority becomes an explosive contributor to the use of drugs. James Kavanaugh describes the problems of these homes in his book, *The Birth of God.*

"Parents insist that their daughter double-date until she is eighteen; they force a son to go to college, or demand that the family spend a vacation together no matter the ages and interest of their children. And if the youngster gets in some kind of trouble, suddenly they decide to play truant officer and private detective. These are the parents who cannot let go, who once disappointed cannot trust, who believe freedom is a commodity suddenly purchased when a child leaves the family home. Sooner or later they are forced to make a choice. Either they must compromise and leave the maturing boy or girl the necessary freedom to make mistakes, or they must create some kind of physical or emotional imprisonment."

Kavanaugh decries ". . . the giant industrial complex which makes a free man punch his timecard and ties him to a steel machine which promises to feed him if he will become an unprotesting slave. Freedom has been defined within the small circle of a religious or political tradition, within the framework of an economic or educational philosophy, so narrow and tight that only a revolution is able to bring about change. The stubborn or helpless are cut off, or excommunicated. The poor and ignorant are starved or ignored. The weak individual is used and manipulated by the strong. The nonconformists are said to be in heresy."

Harsh words? Yes. But to many students they

read like their own indictment on our society. How can we reach these young people? Kavanaugh suggests:

"He will respect the father who wants to know him, who does not smother him with alien goals that seek the honor and praise of the family more than his own honest aspirations. He will not love his father and mother simply because they have given him life and physical sustenance. He demands of them kindness and understanding, honesty and respect. He does not belong to them, he is not some showpiece with which they can win society's applause. . . . He is not afraid to work, to struggle, to go it on his own.

"He does not resent their discipline or honest punishment. . . . He does not admire them for hiding their weaknesses or for refusing to apologize or admit mistakes. . . . He will not accept his parents as perfect, as infallible, as beyond question or recourse. He will not accept material comfort in place of friendship and personal concern. He will not be forced to pay homage to the social emptiness that masquerades as recreation and pleasure. He will make his own mistakes and pay for them. . . . He is himself before he is anyone's child, and he will not give his love where he cannot find respect."

We stress these points because the quality of the home relationship—particularly the relationship a growing adolescent, boy or girl, has with the father—is the biggest single factor in dealing with the problem of drug abuse. Where that relationship is lacking, serious problems can result.

Even in supposedly well-adjusted families, there

are breakdowns in communications and pressures applied from both sides that can only tear down family relationships. Consider some of the techniques teen-agers use on their parents:

1. When they want something, they pout or cry.

2. Threats. "I'm gonna quit school," "I just might get married," and the subtle, "You don't love me or you would . . ."

3. Playing both sides. "Dad won't let me have the car, Mom. Will you ask him for me?"

4. Lies. "I wasn't really involved. I know who took it, but I didn't."

5. Blackmail. "If you make me do it, I'll probably get sick again." "Let me use the car and I'll clean my room . . . or the garage." (Used only in really desperate situations!)

6. Depression. Making life miserable for everybody until the youngster gets his way.

And where did teen-agers learn these techniques? From the example of parents who:

1. Bribe. "Clean your room, and you can buy that new sweater you've been wanting."

2. Use love as a lever. "You wouldn't do this if you loved me."

3. Fake illness. "You'll simply have to quiet down; I think I'm getting a migraine."

4. Make comparisons. "John doesn't get as big an allowance as you do." "Back when I was a boy . . ." "Your brother gets better grades than you."

5. Threats. "If you don't pick up your grandmother, you'll be walking too." "So long as we pay the bills around here, you'd better shape up."

6. Insincere offers. "We'll all go to Catalina . . . Disneyland . . . Yosemite Park . . . someday."

One important element in parent-teen relationships we want to stress here is *listen to your youngsters.* If you wait until junior is on pot to decide it's time to sit down and have a little heart-to-heart talk, you are apt to find the going rough. Many adults insist on always being right . . . on having the last word . . . on being experts in fields where their knowledge may be limited . . . on failing to let their sons and daughters tell them anything. Not that the parent will approve when the youngster is wrong, or take his side against legitimate authority acting fairly, but he should at least begin by listening. This will be a new experience for many parents, and how to get through to adults has to rank as one of the biggest teen-age hangups. An anonymous fifteen-year-old wrote in *Focus on Youth* magazine:

"Some parents don't have the time; therefore, they don't *really* listen to their children. Your parents may be looking right at you, but often their minds are not where their eyes are. It's so frustrating . . . to get a shallow 'uh-huh' after revealing your most challenging discoveries. . . . Sometimes parents listen, but not open-mindedly. They hear you out, then throw it right back at you in a fiery tone of voice. Parents who do listen to what you say often interpret it wrong. This causes a big hassle and makes your parents think their poor little angels are turning into communists, hippies, or some other 'no-no' of society. . . . Some parents could care less about thoughts of their children. 'After all, they're only kids. We will listen to them when they know what they are talking about.' Talking to a parent who wears a blank look on his face is distressing—like talking to a wall. The wall is steep and hard to climb. You keep falling down. To break through this wall is an exciting accomplishment."

Another teen-ager, Leah Stewart of New York City, was looking for friends when she found help at *Encounter, Inc.* She gave the readers of *Focus on Youth* some good insights on parent-teen relationships as they relate to the drug problem:

"When I was sixteen, I was in big trouble. For two years I had used pot, pills, LSD, ether—anything I could find—in my desperate search for some kind of happiness, some release from the constant pain of living. Then, suddenly, I got busted. I thought, *Oh, no, it's all over, I'm lost.* But what actually happened was I found a group of people who helped me slowly, slowly relearn what it meant to be alive, to love, to be loved, and to feel self-esteem. It's a high a million times better than a high.

"What would you have done if you had met me two years ago? Would you have realized I was lonely, confused, in pain? Or figured I was just another supposedly happy-go-lucky hippie? Let me give you some guidelines from my experience because there are an awful lot of things you can do to help a kid like me.

"First, one's behavior always gives him away. If I'm flunking out of school, taking drugs, withdrawing from people, or lying a lot, things just can't be going groovy with me, no matter how much I insist they are. It's up to you, if you are responsible, to confront me strongly about my behavior. Point out how stupid it is, and suggest how I can behave differently. If you feel angry or indignant at me, by all means *show* it—in such a way, of course, as to let me know that it springs from genuine concern for me. That's what will make me change. And a change in behavior is the first crucial step. If I act like a deadhead, people will relate to me as a deadhead, and I'll soon feel like a deadhead, right? So I must reverse the process, i.e., stop acting like a deadhead. Sometimes to get me to do that you will have not only to confront me but to threaten me with serious consequences if you find I haven't stopped.

"Second, once I'm acting like a human being again, I'll need you more than ever. You have the experience to help me deal with all the new problems and situations I'm no longer copping out of. If, for example, I had a weight problem and were slimming down, I'd probably be scared silly at the prospect of being pretty, going out on dates, and having to face all the ensuing problems. But before I can accept your advice and concern, I must trust you. To get me to do that, you must not pretend to be infallible, or to love everything about me, or to know all the answers. No. All you have to be is human. Which means you get just as hurt, angry, tired, jealous, and scared as I do; only you have more experience in dealing with those feelings and situations than I have. If, even after I've realized this, it's still pretty clear I don't wholly trust you, you'd better ask why. And if my reasons seem valid, maybe you'll have to do a little changing, too!

"Third, in order to help me deal with the reasons for my former bad behavior so that I don't fall right back into it, you should be talking to me a lot about emotions. Emotions seem to me to be the gist of people, the basis for all thought and actions. How can anyone who feels rotten all the time ever lead a successful life? Love, guilt, fear, anger, hurt, loneliness, and jealousy are emotions. . . . To be able to recognize and communicate feelings, even the wholly irrational ones like anger over a tiny incident, is most important. This is why you should insist I delve deep into my gut and figure out exactly what it is I'm feeling.

"Fourth, once I begin to do that, you can help me *deal* with my feelings. The rule here is that bad feelings are to be dumped, good ones are to be cherished, and both are to be shared with friends. If I have just been dropped by a boy, chances are I'll be both hurt and angry at him. To dump the bad feeling, I should be encouraged both to cry and get mad, while you (or another close friend) are with me. Not alone in bed at night. Stress that. Stress too that the strongest man is the one who is not afraid to cry and be human, and the most womanly woman is the one who has the guts to stand up for herself. It is simply human to experience emotions, and to deny recognition and outlet to any single one of them is asking to be emotionally disturbed. Guilt and jealousy can be dumped by confessing them to the person I feel guilty and jealous about; loneliness by crying with someone who cares for me; fear by getting angry at whatever it is I'm afraid of, and/or asking people for a lot of support before doing the scary thing. Good feelings, like love and joy, are maintained only by spreading them: loving others, giving them joy. Joy and love I can keep only by giving them away.

"Fifth, the last step consists of your being aware of my misconceptions. Question my values so I can learn to question them myself. Make sure I am not pursuing wealth, social status, or intellectuality to the exclusion of happiness, friendship, and love. Make sure I know to do only rarely that which makes me even remotely sorry afterwards. Show me how to be honest and open, and confront me when I start sliding. Straighten up my misunderstandings about sex . . . and a million other matters.

"When, after getting rid of all the bad feelings, attitudes, and patterns of behavior, I begin to feel good enough about myself to interact freely with others, life gets pretty exciting. Beautiful, even!"

Dr. William Nesbitt, a private practitioner with a special interest in psychiatry who has worked closely with the Haight-Ashbury Medical Clinic, has some good advice for parents:

"Let us not go astray in dealing with half-truths or falsehoods about drugs, and in so doing turn off our young generation completely. Let us in all honesty present the scientific facts and the abundance of living in cooperation with God's design for us. . . . Whatever the outcome of our involvement with the drug scene we personally will be the better for tuning in. Why? Because tuning in means we must take seriously the call to slow down, to live our lives instead of enduring them, to open our eyes and really see what is happening around us and in us, to respond to beauty, to humanize our large-scale social structures."

Dr. David Smith agrees with this counsel and adds some advice of his own for parents in *Focus on Youth*:

"Parents I have talked with are hysterical, and their position is that all drug use must stop at all costs. It is almost impossible to ease the minds of adults unless they are willing to look at the facts objectively and to reconsider their old attitudes, many of which have sprung out of erroneous information. Unless we are willing to become totally honest we will only increase the drug problem rather than alleviate it.

"One night recently when I was working late a mother dragged her distraught nineteen-year-old down to the clinic with a stomach ache. The girl had been given a ride by some fellow who handed her a cigarette that smelled funny. The mother was convinced the boy had slipped her a marijuana stick. She was obviously certain that marijuana was causing the girl's stomach problem. The girl was sick to her stomach and vomiting; she had stomach flu. The girl had had experience with marijuana before, and knew the cigarette was not marijuana; but she could not tell her mother this. And the mother just went to pieces here in the office. I see this happening and I know the most important advice I can give to parents is to learn as many facts as possible and face them honestly.

"Another suggestion I would like to make to parents is that you save your moralizing and punishment until after the immediate crisis is over. Punishment at the time of crisis actually increases the potentially bad effects of any drug.

"It is also important for parents to realize how tremendous the pressures are on young people to use drugs. Many adults do not understand how boldly our society encourages the idea of drug use to such a degree these days that the teen-ager who does not experiment with drugs is probably the exception. The message of American advertising is, 'cure your pains via chemicals!' Adults set a powerful example—the 'necessary' cigarette, the liquor before dinner, diet pills, sleeping pills, tranquilizers, and so on. Many of these same parents see teen-agers who use drugs as evil fiends, criminals, degenerates. They support stronger . . . laws to punish young people who merely follow in their parents' or society's footsteps. What is a crime is that so many adults ignore the causes of drug abuse and shut their ears to the real concerns of the young. Young people need the facts to make rational decisions about using drugs. Once they have relevant information about drug effects and alternatives to drugs, they usually come up with appropriate conclusions.

". . . the primary motivation for drug use in a younger group is curiosity. If they can't believe what they are hearing, or what they are hearing doesn't make particular sense to them, or they hear nothing, then of course their curiosity is not satisfied at all. These are the ones who most likely move on to experiment for themselves.

"When you are working with young people you have a serious responsibility to provide them with adequate and authoritative drug information. This will equip them to be prepared to make rational decisions about their own drug use."

GOING TO POT

In Chapel Hill, North Carolina, a scientist injects a substance into the tail of a mouse, exposes the tail to hot light and watches to see how long it takes for the animal to react to pain.

In a laboratory in New York, a college student takes a final puff on an odd-looking cigarette, then lies back and closes his eyes while an electroencephalogram scratches out a record of the electrical impulses from his brain.

In Augusta, Georgia, a researcher pumps a liquid into the body of a pregnant rabbit and a week later removes a litter of grossly malformed or dead fetuses.

These are three of the current experiments reported by the *New York Times* as being conducted by scientists in an attempt to unlock the mysteries of marijuana and to answer an increasing social and scientific question: is marijuana safe or harmful, and if it is harmful, how dangerous is it?

Marijuana is an easy-to-grow, easily recognizable plant, with long, narrow, jagged-edged leaflets growing like poorly spaced spokes on a wheel. The plant grows about five feet tall in this country and has a hollow, four-cornered stalk that may reach two inches in diameter.

Generally the plants grown in this country are relatively weak and have a poor taste. Plants from Mexico are about twice as strong, and those from the warm, moist climate of India may be four to five times as potent in their content of the active resin, tetrahydrocannabinol. This is the sticky stuff, found mainly in the flowers and upper leaves, which produces the "marijuana effect." About 95 per cent of the marijuana consumed in the United States comes from Mexico. Since the drug is illegal, its dosage is not and cannot conceivably be standardized. One cannot therefore be certain of the potency of the unlawful prize he has purchased.

Marijuana has been around for a long time. The ancients, as far back as 1200 B.C., used it as a stimulant. It has been considered by some to have analgesic and sedative qualities. It has many names and is grown the world over. Commercially, it is used to manufacture rope and a cloth similar to burlap.

Growing, transporting, and dealing in marijuana is a $100,000,000 a year illegal industry. Contrary to popular belief, the Mafia never has been involved in marijuana traffic. The product has been too bulky, too difficult to handle, the profit margin too small. (It takes no more ingenuity to smuggle a pound of heroin than it does a pound of marijuana, and a pound of heroin will retail for $50,000, while a pound of pot will usually bring no more than $100.)

The marijuana trade traditionally has been the prerogative of small, independent operators. The traffic across the United States-Mexican border has been loose and unstructured, involving college students, small-time underworld elements, and ordinary citizens of the United States and Mexico who are members of neither one group nor the other. In a recent twelve-month period, United States Customs and Border Patrol agents seized twelve tons of marijuana being smuggled from Tijuana, Mexico, into southern California. They are aided in their work by dogs carefully trained to sniff out the pot and by a network of informers, including many sellers south of the border, who are eager for the reward given for smuggling information.

Marijuana can be transported loose or compressed into "bricks." The bricks are most common and weigh one kilo (2.2 pounds). A kilo can be purchased in Mexico for $40 to $50 and sold in the United States for $100 or more depending on the quality, current demand, and distance from the border. Kilos are divided into one-pound and one-ounce packages for further distribution. These are usually wrapped in plastic sandwich bags. A one-ounce quantity is referred to as a "lid" and usually will sell for $10. One lid will produce from fifty to one hundred finished cigarettes depending on the quality of the marijuana and the desired cigarette size. A finished marijuana joint will cost anywhere from three for $1.00 to $1.50 each. Ordinary hand-roll cigarette papers are used for this purpose, but it is relatively simple to distinguish marijuana from tobacco. Marijuana will not pack together, so both ends of a joint must be rolled tight to prevent loss. Marijuana burns with a brighter glow than tobacco, must be kept ignited by constant puffing, and has a sweet odor often compared to burning rope.

In processing prior to sale, the leaves and flowering tops of the plant are stripped off and dried. This drying process usually is carried out in the shade because direct sunlight causes the material to turn brown. This dried, rough material must then have the stems, twigs, and seeds removed, a laborious hand process known as "manicuring."

Because of their expense, marijuana sticks are smoked down to a tiny butt called a "roach." This is done with the assistance of a "crutch" which may be an electrical alligator clip, a wire formed into a holder, or simply a matchbook cover rolled around a reefer.

The use of marijuana is difficult to detect. The person using it may frequently have reddened eyes but not dilated pupils. In early stages of use, the person may be stimulated or behave in a silly fashion. Later on, he may be very sleepy or stuporous. There are no blood or urine tests to detect its use.

Because use of grass can be difficult to prove conclusively, some students actually smoke in school and attend classes in glassy-eyed contentment. Los Gatos, California, High School reports that 578 of their 1,570 students (37 percent) smoke marijuana practically every weekend and also on at least three of the other five days of the week—more students than use tobacco in this particular school.

There is also widespread use of synthetic pot, THC—tetrahydrocannibinol, sometimes called Delta

One, the active intoxicant in the pungent resin that oozes from the flowering tops and leaves of the female *Cannabis sativa* plant. This active principle of marijuana was first identified in 1966 by an Israeli chemist, Dr. Rafael Mechoulam, and later developed into an economical synthesis by Dr. Edward C. Taylor and a chemical research team at Princeton University. The United States Bureau of Narcotics and Dangerous Drugs is seriously concerned by reports that organized crime may be planning to produce and market synthetic marijuana on a vast scale.

The big question with marijuana, of course, is its effects on the growing number of high school and college students using it—and that use is now reaching down into the junior high and even elementary grade levels.

A report to the Superior Court in the State of Massachusetts listed these findings on marijuana:

1. The drug's only purpose is to induce intoxication. Users tend to become advocates of the drug among nonusers.

2. The effects of marijuana, as noted, are not predictable and depend on the psychological susceptibility of the user who suffers mind disorientation and impaired perception and coordination.

3. A user tends to be emotionally unstable and can be unpredictably violent. His personal habits and appearance change.

Pot parties are not uncommon among students. Several smokers congregate in a room, automobile, or other small space offering little or no ventilation. A joint is passed among the users who drag deeply, hold the smoke in their lungs as long as possible, then exhale slowly. As more joints are added to the ritual, the room fills with smoke and is rebreathed by the users. Soon they will feel high, much as if they had several cocktails. Time, space, and sounds then take on new and unusual dimensions.

The marijuana produces a euphoric sense of well-being in the user. It also seems to heighten emotions; but in some users this progresses quickly to irritability, excitability, and even violence. Judgment frequently is impaired.

"It is virtually incontrovertible that for the unstable person marijuana can lead to neurosis, psychosis, and irrational or undesirable behavior," according to Dr. Donald B. Louria, head of the New York State Council on Drug Addiction.

"While marijuana acts as a sedative-hallucinogen for most people, it does cause certain other individuals to become combatant and aggressive. Some of these have been reported to have become homicidal or suicidal," reports Dr. Lindsay R. Curtis in *Listen* magazine.

"Let's be honest," Dr. Curtis continues. "Marijuana is not addicting in the sense that heroin or opiates are addicting. There is no physical effect upon withdrawal of the drug, even after prolonged usage. There is no craving. Yet there is a type of emotional drug dependence that seems effectively to invite the user back again and again so that he continues to use the drug."

Dr. David Smith points out some of the dangers of marijuana in *Focus on Youth*:

"Obviously, the immediate danger is intoxication. You have less impairment of the motor function than you do with alcohol intoxication, but you have more impairment of perceptual function—how you perceive time and space, how you react to your environment through all your senses.

"Second, individuals who smoke marijuana daily to the point of intoxication develop what I define as the amotivational syndrome. For example, in the Bay Area (San Francisco and surrounding communities) 35 percent of the high school students in grades nine through twelve have smoked marijuana one or more times. They may use it one time experimentally. They may use it periodically for parties. Or they may abuse it to the point where they are stoned most of the day—these are the kids who have a joint on the way to school, one at lunchtime, another in the locker room, and another on the way home. This kind of person has become known as a pot head. His amotivational syndrome shows up through a deterioration of his grades, and a reduction of his motivation to participate in any sort of complex or futuristic act."

Does marijuana have any potential medical value? Not likely, in the opinion of Dr. Donald B. Louria. In his book *The Drug Scene,* Dr. Louria comments, ". . . on the basis of past data there is little reason to believe *cannabis* preparations will play any significant role in medical therapeutics in the future."

Dr. Louria also comments on the comparison between marijuana and alcohol:

"The proponents for legalization of marijuana not only demand the comparison be made but insistently point out that alcohol is a dangerous drug which is perfectly legal in our society. . . . To argue for marijuana on the grounds that it is no more dangerous than alcohol is, of course, a totally negative approach. . . . Surely alcohol is a dangerous drug. . . . The question is simply whether we are to add to our alcohol burden another intoxicant. In the United States there is currently a death from automobile accidents approximately every eleven minutes and an injury every eighteen seconds. Shall we add another intoxicant such as marijuana, increase the number of inebriated drivers or pedestrians, and attain a death rate of perhaps one every eight minutes or even every five minutes and an injury every twelve seconds or every eight seconds? Surely society must have the right, indeed the obligation, to control its escape mechanisms and intoxicants."

Though marijuana is not a narcotic, medically speaking, it is usually so treated under federal law and the laws of the various states. The possession of grass can be a felony, punishable in some jurisdictions by prison terms of from one to ten years, or more. There is currently considerable study going on by both federal and state authorities, as well as in Canada, to reexamine the severe penalties for the use of marijuana. But still, any young person who would risk an arrest record for a night of kicks would have to be a fool.

There is a great deal more we need to learn about marijuana and its effects. And we may get some of those answers. The National Institute of Mental Health is supporting twenty-four research projects on marijuana alone and thirty-two others that include marijuana among several drugs being studied.

The institute has allocated about $1 million for marijuana research, of which almost half is being spent to grow marijuana and synthesize THC for experimental use.

Testifying before a committee of the United States House of Representatives, Dr. Stanley F. Yolles, director of the National Institute for Mental Health, said these new studies show marijuana interferes with the thinking process and recent memory, weakens concentration, and "subtly" retards speech. It also was found to stimulate anxieties and guilt feelings, but, contrary to reputation, tends to turn a person inward rather than stimulate "conviviality," he said.

Many students continue to use marijuana, oblivious to the possible physical and mental dangers and willing to take whatever legal risks may continue to be involved from such use.

Others have changed their minds. One young man wrote to newspaper columnist Ann Landers:

"I am twenty, male, and have been smoking pot since I was seventeen. I've heard a lot of weird stories and I'm sure most of the stories are exaggerated to scare kids off. Some of my friends have been smoking for five years and have had no bad effects. Others have gotten into all kinds of trouble. I'm convinced it all depends on the physical condition of the smoker and how strong the stuff is. I got off pot seven weeks ago and I hope you will print my letter because it might help somebody.

"Six months after I started to smoke I began to get terrific headaches which lasted two and three days. Then I developed a sort of sleeping sickness.

I could fall asleep any place, any time, in any position.

"When I started to fall asleep on the highway I decided I'd better quit, but I kept going back to the joints because I liked the feeling. Pot smokers tell each other it is not habit forming but I'd like to know what you call it when you can't quit.

"Two months ago I was high from a smoke and decided to drive to a town only twenty-two miles away. The next thing I knew I was in the hospital. I had fallen asleep at the wheel and hit an abutment. The car was demolished. I was lucky to get out alive, and lucky that I didn't kill a carful of people.

"I thank God I got off pot before it wrecked my life. I'd sign my name but my folks would die of the shock. . . ."

Another young man who decided too much was more than enough is a high school senior. When Mark was a freshman he was active in sports and student government as well as getting good grades. He was curious about pot and easily influenced by older students whom he admired. He went from using one joint now and then to being a regular user. In the process he quickly lost interest in his studies and activities. He was picked up one night for possession and released later by the juvenile court on probation. The experience was enough to make him think . . . and quit.

He's recovering much of the ground he lost in school, but it's a long, hard battle.

Go back to pot? "No, thank you," Mark replies, "not for me. I've been that route. Kids who go to pot . . . go to pot!"

. . . and many experts agree. Dr. Edward Bloomquist of the University of Southern California and author of the book, *Marijuana,* comments, "Kids who get high repeatedly don't want to come down. They don't want to do anything else. They find a world where they seemingly have no problems, and they become social bums . . . marijuana is an unpredictable drug used by unpredictable people with unpredictable results."

A TIGER IN
YOUR BLOODSTREAM

It's difficult to imagine Art Linkletter in any other role than the happy, friendly entertainer who for many years has entered millions of homes by way of radio and television.

But Art is very serious as he discusses the death of his daughter, Diane, age twenty, who plunged from the kitchen window of a Hollywood apartment while under the influence of LSD. Linkletter says her fatal plunge was the result of taking "a tiger in her bloodstream."

Linkletter often lectures at colleges on the permissiveness of our society which he feels encourages drug use. "I intend to re-emphasize that point. I think my daughter's death is going to be paid for many, many times by the kind of things I can say and get done, using this as an example," he says.

"I've been as good a parent as I could possibly be, I think. We've been a very close family. My wife and I have tried to set a good example. We have tried to keep our children up-to-date on what the dangerous things are, but perhaps we did not bear down as hard as we should have.

". . . Diane, of all the children, was always the most daring. She was the most emotionally up and down. She was either on top of the mountain or in the valley of despair—over trivial things."

Diane became an actress, so her father was not too surprised at reports that she might be going with a group that was experimenting around.

"I brought it out, as I do everything," he explains. "Our lines of communication were open as far as I was concerned. I said, 'Diane, is it true this group has been experimenting with some of the new things?' And she admitted that it was.

"I pointed out the obvious dangers. She agreed, and with consummate skill acted out the part that she would never do it again. Obviously she did it again. Over the months she found she had a tiger in her bloodstream.

"Apparently what finally happened was that she became despondent over a spat with her boyfriend and took a much stronger dose of this poison than she should have. She was worried that she would never come out of it mentally, and this led to her death.

"I want the parents and I want their kids to read about this and be shocked, be frightened at what can happen.

"When somebody like Timothy Leary comes out and justifies it, we have got to jump on him with hobnailed boots. Such people are casting doubt on the authority of people who know how deadly these things can be.

"Those kids I've talked to who use it tell me that when you're on what they call a trip, with a heavy dose of LSD, every one of your faults and shortcomings stands out in stark-naked, unrelieved, unrationalized relief. There is no place to hide.

"We know of a college girl who was fed a sugar cube with heavy LSD at a cocktail party by fraternity guys as a joke, and she didn't even know she had taken it. She didn't know there was anything on the cube. She was just taking a tidbit. This was three years ago, and she is still at U.C.L.A. in a ward, practically a vegetable.

"If I can save a few lives . . ." Linkletter didn't finish the sentence.

There is a tremendous need for parents, teachers, and counselors as well as young people themselves to learn the true facts about drugs. Words like *addiction, trip, high, hallucinate,* and *flashback* have become basic vocabulary for a drug-oriented generation. But not every young person knows specifically what those words mean, and many adults are even more lacking in their knowledge. Tragedies, such as happened to Art Linkletter's daughter, and incidents in their own communities are causing many parents to believe drug tragedies just might happen to them and their families. What kinds of drugs are being used? What are the symptoms? What should a parent or concerned friend do?

There often are symptoms *before* drug use starts, and there are a number to note after involvement with various drugs. A young person who is straight may, because of peer pressure, pick up the idea drugs aren't so bad, start justifying their use, and identify with the drug-using crowd. This is an early symptom that often appears before any drug use actually takes place.

Then, as a youngster starts using drugs, look for a change in his ideas, attitudes, ambition, appearance, and personality—not necessarily all of these, or big changes, or all at once—but look for them.

Watch for a sudden drop in grades and a loss of interest in sports and extracurricular activities. The young person will become passive or begin to enjoy a dreamy, way-out form of art and music along with a questionable group of companions.

There are a number of different types of drugs students use, and that list is constantly changing and being added to. About the most dangerous are the stimulants, primarily the amphetamines, which stimulate the central nervous system. They are known for their ability to combat fatigue and sleepiness and, as a diet curb, are basic to many weight-reduction programs. Amphetamines are known as pep pills, wake-ups, eyeopeners, copilots, truck drivers, beans, or bennies. As with other dangerous drugs, the slang names applied to them by users frequently are derived from the shapes and colors of the capsules or tablets, their effect, or their use.

Among the most common pep pills used by teenagers are benzedrine tablets or *bennies*. They are round, white, and marked diagonally. Also widely used is methedrine, sometimes called crystal, crank, or speed, and comes in either powder or liquid form.

A young person will take an amphetamine either orally or by injection. The flash or rush feeling is much greater and faster with the needle, and he can develop a pleasant feeling of euphoria known as a high. In this state he is alert, excitable, and has a seemingly large reserve of power and mental alertness on which he can draw. For this reason many students use these pep pills when staying up late to study for an examination or in other situations calling for an extra amount of stamina. There is great danger of producing psychological dependence whereby the user feels a big letdown when not using his "upper."

Besides some of the previously mentioned symptoms, a person on amphetamines will be restless, talkative, perspire heavily, have enlarged pupils, loss of appetite, weight loss, and, if amphetamines are continued for a long period, can develop high blood pressure, abnormal heart rhythms, and, possibly, suicidal tendencies (if he is in a low state when without the drug).

Mr. Bowen was called by one mother whose freshman son was on barbiturates, a downer, in this instance *reds*, seconal tablets. The boy had an I.Q. of over 140 and had been introduced to the drug scene with some marijuana joints.

His mother was aware he had been using drugs, but thought it was just a phase he was going through, and that he wouldn't go beyond the use of marijuana. But he went to the amphetamines, in his case, bennies. Then he switched to a speed run for a couple of weeks, and began a deep depression, a serious and regular symptom of amphetamine use. Like many junior and senior high school students, Dan just didn't know how to combat the low, depressive moods he was encountering after he came down from his highs.

Dan wrote a suicide note to his parents and went out and obtained eleven seconal tablets. He had taken five of them when his mother came into his room, noticed he was unconscious, and called Mr. Bowen. By the time a doctor arrived, Dan was in a coma and was rushed to the hospital. He nearly died. Later he spent several weeks in a mental hospital working out some of the feelings he just could not control. He insisted to Mr. Bowen and the doctors that in his depressed state, suicide was his only way out. He later was released but has had a rocky road back to a somewhat normal pattern of living.

In another experience, several high school football players started using benzedrine before the games because they had heard that some of the great college and pro athletes do. At first they took them before the game on Fridays, then they backed up to Thursdays to get ready, and finally they used them before each practice session. Some real guilt feelings developed. Mr. Bowen got these fellows together, and for the first time they saw the dangers involved. There *is* a pleasant high to be obtained with these stimulants, and a feeling of more power, but the depression that follows can be devastating. Being moody and having red and runny eyes doesn't make for better sports ability either.

Mark started on speed when he was in the ninth grade. An older brother and several of his relatives and friends were members of the drug crowd, and he didn't want to be left out. He wasn't. He started off with small hits and worked his way up to the point where he was hitting the needle four or five times a day as a "speed freak." In six months, his weight had dropped, and his face was thin and hollow. He had contracted infectious hepatitis, and he was very familiar with the cold chills, stomach cramps, and sores that are part of the drug life.

Fortunately—and he says this himself—he was caught and eventually sent to the county ranch where he had a chance to take a good look at himself. With some counseling, he began to think of a new direction for his life. He chose to go in the service when his release was due rather than to risk returning to the crowd, the street, and the drugs. The battle for personal freedom was too big a one to surrender to the needle.

And there are the depressants or barbiturates: the reds that Dan took; the sedatives and sleeping pills; seconal, phenobarbital, nebutal, etc. They are available as liquids, tablets, or capsules and are called candy, goofballs, or by their color as capsules: yellows, pinks, blue birds, or rainbows. They also are known as red devils and double trouble.

Barbiturates produce impaired judgment, slow reaction timing, slurring of speech, staggering, loss of balance, a quarrelsome disposition, and sometimes a coma, with danger of pneumonia and death. Combined with alcohol they are even more dangerous. They produce physical dependence and require a withdrawal far more dangerous than the withdrawal from narcotics, for it produces nervousness, headaches, anxiety, nausea, changes in blood pressure, mental confusion, delirium, hallucinations, and possibly a coma.

Like the amphetamines, barbiturates have a

definite legitimate medical use, but in the hands of the amateur they are dangerous and deadly.

A youngster on reds, for example, can be spotted in the classroom when he acts like a person highly intoxicated on alcohol. He may try to fake his way out by saying he was up late the night before, but prolonged or serious symptoms should invite more investigation.

Curiosity can lead to problems. Mr. Bowen received a call late one night after a basketball game to visit a youngster who was stoned on seconal and was afraid he was going to die. When Mr. Bowen went to the house, the boy had calmed considerably and said he didn't really think he was going to die; he had just been scared by an unpleasant and first probe into the world of drugs. He had feelings with which he just could not cope. He had been straight all his life and had been conned by other teens into turning on—the chemical cop-out.

One form of getting high that attracts many younger students is glue sniffing. If glue is not available they will settle for paint thinner, hair spray, or gasoline. The effects on the body are similar to that of a general anesthetic: a tingling sensation in the head, lightness, and an exhilaration called a *jag*. Quick-drying plastic cement, used in model airplane glue, can be very harmful when breathed. It produces dizziness, slurred speech, staggering, irritability, rash, and even unconsciousness. Because it results in one of the fastest and most dangerous highs of any of the drugs, manufacturers recently have started adding horseradish to their glue which certainly serves to lessen its appeal as an inhalant! The glue sniffer commonly has inflamed eyes, loses appetite and weight, and feels constantly sick. Prolonged use may lead to liver, brain, and kidney damage as well as to destruction of bone marrow.

A fifth-grade student told Mr. Bowen about breathing gasoline. The boy would take a gallon of gasoline, place it under his bed, run a tube up under his pillow, and lie awake breathing the fumes. He said one night, after breathing the gasoline for awhile, he saw the door open, and two very small, red men with long antennae came walking through it. This hallucination scared him—but not enough to make him quit his nocturnal sniffing. His parents were completely unaware of his activities.

Another student inhaled excessive quantities of a spray used for cough control, got stoned, and experienced vivid hallucinations. Later he suffered a loss of memory, developed a passive attitude, his grades fell, and it was some time before he was able to function normally again.

There are a number of hallucinatory drugs, one of the best known being d-lysergic acid diethylamide tartrate, better known as LSD 25, or acid. LSD is tasteless, odorless, and colorless. When taken even in the smallest quantity it is likely to cause the mind to react in strange, unpredictable and uncontrollable ways. As little as 1/25 millionth of an ounce may produce symptoms such as hallucinations, distortion of color and sound perception, panic, personality changes, loss of sanity, impulses towards violence, impulses toward suicidal acts, psychosis, or any combination of these. The effects are totally unpredictable and vary widely from person to person and trip to trip. They may last from eight to twelve hours and may recur at a later date without the person taking the drug again (a flashback). There is documented evidence of malformed babies of white mice after the mother had been given LSD in the gestation period. There is also evidence of genes and chromosomes damage to the human white blood cells. Further studies are now being undertaken to determine the correlation of genetic damage in humans resulting from the use of LSD.

Dr. Thomas Ungerlieder and his staff at the U.C.L.A. neuro-psychiatric center have treated many young patients who have used LSD. He introduced Mr. Bowen to one young patient who appeared normal but who was constantly hallucinating although it had been several months since his bad LSD trip. He was convinced there was a plot by underworld agents to destroy the hospital.

Mr. McLean met a high school junior who had attacked his sister-in-law, stabbing her with scissors while on an LSD trip. Another young high school athlete had run down the street naked under the influence of the drug. A third youth had been pulled off the hood of a car he had leaped onto at a busy intersection while hallucinating on acid. These events may be isolated, but they add further to the damning evidence against LSD.

Dr. Ungerlieder points out there are many unanswered questions on LSD. For example, doctors do not know why flashbacks continue, or why only some patients have them, or the reason for the varying degrees of intensity.

As well as bad mental effects, LSD causes dilated pupils, increased blood pressure, nausea, chills, irregular breathing, trembling, and loss of sleep while the trip lasts. In fact, the pupils are so widely dilated the user frequently protects his eyes with dark glasses.

Despite this list of symptoms, it is not always easy to tell if a young person is using acid: a user may exhibit all or hardly any of them.

A unique aspect of LSD use is the missionary zeal with which some users whose trips have been pleasant and exciting will approach their friends and urge them to use it. They can be highly persuasive, persistent, and effective in getting others to turn on.

But despite their arguments, the drug, at this point, is too dangerous and unpredictable for any legitimate medical use and its manufacture and distribution is illegal.

Narcotics—or, medically speaking, the drugs that are opiates—originally came from the opium poppy or are derivatives. Included are morphine, codine, heroin, paragoric, and opium itself. Synthetic substitutes include demerol and methedon.

Heroin, often known as *H* or *horse*, is by far the most widely-used narcotic. Production is prohibited in America. It is not now used even for medical purposes. Heroin must be cut or diluted, and the user has no way of knowing how accurately this has been done. Overdoses and death often result from heroin use. H has a particularly powerful depressant action on the respiratory system and produces such side effects as constipation, loss of appetite, impotency or sterility, and can produce a stupor or even a coma. The use of narcotics develops both physical and psychological dependency. A tolerance builds up rapidly, calling for ever-increasing amounts. Because of this, the chances of addiction are great. Users often are hooked before they realize it.

Lasting cures are few. Less than 10 percent of heroin addicts ever successfully kick the habit; the rest usually end in jail or die as derelicts. Dr. Donald Louria, president of the New York State Council on Drug Addiction, predicts that before long "every high school and every college in the country will be inundated by heroin." Another expert foresees that 40 to 60 percent of elementary students soon will be frequent users of marijuana and hard drugs.

Withdrawal from the use of narcotics is severe. Very few permanent cures are recorded. The cost of supporting the increased demand frequently forces the user into various criminal acts to finance his supply.

Fortunately most students are afraid of heroin, but its use on the secondary school level is becoming more frequent. The heroin available to adults comes from either Mexico or France, the French variety being preferred. Before use, it is diluted in either milk sugar or glucose. The original supply has been cut a number of times and the price raised as it has been passed down the network of suppliers.

Cy is a young man from lower middle-class background who decided early that the Merchant Marine was more to his liking than the classroom. As he visited Hong Kong and other Asian ports, he soon saw the opportunity to make big money by trafficking in drugs. At first he didn't want to use any, but later he found he had to. "I had to taste it or snort a little to make sure I was really getting the good stuff," he told Mr. Bowen. "A seller will often burn you any chance he gets. I wasn't aware I was hooked until one day at sea I started going through withdrawal symptoms." The amount of time it takes to get hooked will vary a great deal. For Cy it took quite awhile.

To supplement his selling income, Cy became an accomplished thief, but even this talent could not meet his ever-growing needs. With the assistance of his wife, a registered nurse, he decided to try to kick the habit.

"Is the monkey still on your back?" Mr. Bowen asked him.

"No, it really isn't. I feel I'm cured of heroin, but it's been a miserable battle every inch of the way. I'm kind of lucky. I'm one of the few guys I ever knew to make it." Cy is busy now working with other young men caught up in the drug scene.

As a medicinal pain killer, an opiate is effective. As a tyrant running loose, it is deadly. It is a chain too weak to be felt until it is too strong to be broken.

On the teen-age level, rock festivals around the country often become one big drug turn-on. At such an event recently, "peace pills" were thrown into a crowd of unsuspecting teen-agers. Nine young people ended up in the hospital. The pill was actually a tranquilizer used to sedate vicious animals. Other youngsters tell of parties where many of the kids bring drugs, put them in a large container, then swallow whatever each draws out! One thing is sure —kids who will do this certainly are not afraid of drugs. Also popular at parties are mescaline (a hallucinogenic chemical found in the buttons of a small cactus plant—peyote or mescal—which also is supplied illegally as a powder or liquid) and psilocybin (a mind-influencing drug which comes in crystal, powder or liquid form, and originates with a Mexican mushroom). STP (also known as DOM) is fairly new on the scene. It is a synthetic chemical related to mescaline and the amphetamines. It is reported to be extremely mind-distorting.

Where do the drugs come from? The major sources of supply are either underground chemical labs or the excess supply from legitimate manufacturers which is bootlegged to a ready market. An estimated ten billion capsules and dangerous tablets are produced every year in this country, and it is believed more than half of that quantity finds its way into the hands of drug abusers through illegal channels.

How do drugs actually get onto the high school campus? Drugs are coming onto the campus through students themselves. They are traded, sold, and sometimes given free. Some students make just enough for their own supply. Others handle a much larger volume. One young high school junior sold nearly $10,000 worth of drugs in four months on and near his campus. He had regular clients, took orders, and kept books!

Behind the young campus supplier is an adult, often a member of the underworld syndicates, eager for greedy gain off the weaknesses of youth.

One interesting pusher went by the name of Dr. Zoom—doctor because he often stole drugs to cure the physical illnesses of his addict friends, and zoom because he was frequently on amphetamine runs. His real name is Russ, and he has tried every possible kind of drug in his nine years as a user and dealer. He also manufactured many of the drugs including a new one called peanut butter speed, named from its color in the manufacturing process. He assured us he would never sell to high school students. "That's beneath my professional dignity!" he said. It may be, but most other sellers have no such scruples and find teen-agers an easy prey and market.

Another young seller—on a four-year cycle of busts, jail, treatment, and use—told us, "I can't quit, I'll probably be in it until I die." Did he think he'd be alive in a few years? "No," he replied. "But the greatest way to go is with an overdose of H."

Among other things, parents should find out if a youngster is involved with drugs because of curiosity or experimentation as distinguished from some underlying problem. It is easy for parents to overreact. This can be as bad as no concern at all.

One very attractive ninth grade girl tried one marijuana joint, and her parents found out. They grounded her for one year. The girl got so frustrated, and communication broke down so badly, she eventually sneaked out without her parents' knowledge and went on to try different kinds of drugs out of rebellion and spite.

A youngster needs to know his parents love him even if they don't always approve of his conduct.

The problem of drugs, like other problems of adolescence, is best faced in an atmosphere of calmness, understanding, and reasoning. Professional help from a counselor, teacher, physician, or pastor can always supplement the efforts of the parents themselves. When these fail, the police and the juvenile authorities may have to be brought in to keep a young person from destroying himself.

Young people need help with the decision-making process, and encouragement will go a lot further than anger or threats. Life values never are learned automatically. They are taught by precept and example, by kindness and firmness.

If a youngster uses drugs for experimentation, he needs to be given facts on what they can do to him medically, socially, and legally.

If he has succumbed to peer pressure, he needs to be strengthened in his motivation, and his own worth as a person reassessed.

And if he has simply sought hedonistic pleasure, you're dealing with a moral and spiritual vacuum that can be solved only by coming to grips with those lacks in his life—and perhaps in his family's.

Education *is* important. Young people need to know the possibilities of brain damage, loss of memory, chromosome damage—facts that any adult talking to a teen-ager should make a point to know, and know accurately. You—and they—should know the difference between marijuana, amphetamines, barbiturates, opiates, and hallucinogens. They should be told about the dubious quality of black-marketed, bootlegged drugs and the unpredictablility of various effects.

But education alone is not the answer. In the final analysis, the God-given right of individual choice will be exercised no matter how compelling the facts. But a kind, knowledgeable, understanding, patient adult can do much to influence the direction at that turning point.

DRUGS AND THE SCHOOLS

With the drug problem looming large almost overnight in most parts of the country, school officials often did not know what to do or where to turn for answers. Few schools had adequate courses of instruction on the drugs and their effects; fewer still had teachers equipped with sufficient knowledge and rapport to effectively communicate in this area with students.

"Any indictment of the schools and colleges on their behavior in the field is fair," comments Dr. Louria in a statement quoted in *Newsweek*. "They have failed to face the real problems of drug abuse. . . ."

Then there was the issue of what to do with students caught either using or furnishing marijuana, dangerous drugs, or narcotics. Some schools ignored the problem only to see it get worse, while others expelled any student even under suspicion, which only added to hostilities.

One school principal was unhappy over published reports of drug abuse among his student body, so he called the press in and flatly told them he knew of no student on his campus using any illegal drug. Within two weeks, fifty students on his campus had been arrested on various drug charges. They included a student body officer, a top athlete, the girl who was secretary in the principal's office, and the boy who dated his daughter!

Classroom strategy was often as unrealistic. Out-of-date drug movies, lectures from medical and legal authorities, and instruction from teachers who knew less about the drugs in question than students in the class hurt the cause more than they helped.

The Campbell High School district in San Jose was really not any better off than the rest of the high schools as far as being prepared for a skyrocketing menace, but the district did face up to its needs and tried to take some constructive steps.

Developing a total approach to the problem—classroom, counseling, discipline, and community cooperation—would take the services of a knowledgeable man. The district didn't have one, so they decided to make their own expert, Haskell Bowen.

"Hack," as he is popularly known, is a health educator and a basketball coach. He had related to young people closely and well during his thirteen years in the district. He knew little about drugs, but was asked to take a year's time to learn all he could about the problem.

The assignment was interesting and a real challenge. He accepted it, and over a period of time was to have at his fingertips a great deal of knowledge and experience from which to guide his school colleagues. During the year, he had some interesting experiences, met experts in the field all across the nation, talked to thousands of young people in the back seat of police cars, in juvenile detention, on campuses, at treatment centers, and on the streets. As young people got to know and trust him, he would get calls for help at all hours of the day and night. Out of his work came a teaching guide for classroom use and a realistic concept of both the responsibility and direction a local school system should take in meeting the drug problem.

He worked closely with the Narcotics Detail of the San Jose Police Department. His daily companions were Sergeants Larry Stuefloton, Don Trujillo, Bobby Burrows, and Glen Terry. His first days with the squad were spent on adult cases only. Hack was shown how a drug raid was set up and was amazed at the widespread use of the real hard narcotics—the opiates, heroin, and morphine— that rarely are found among high school students but are used in great quantity by many young adults.

He saw some of the investigating techniques used by the officers. He watched them testify in court, and learned about the search and seizure laws. Then he was given opportunity to work directly with high school students under investigation and was amazed at the openness with which many of these young people talk if they feel they can really level with someone they trust.

There were times when Hack wished he was back in the safe and pleasant surroundings of a high school classroom. At least one police raid offered more than casual adventure, and Hack later described it to one of his classes:

It was a wet, cold afternoon when a call was received from a motel owner in south San Jose who suspected there was drug usage in his motel. With Sergeants Ron Utts and Glen Terry, I got in a squad car and drove to the motel. The owner met us as we pulled into the driveway and said, "There have been two girls using one of the rooms, and last night we became very concerned because fifteen men were in and out all night long. Then the girls left early this morning—without paying. As we went in to clean up the room, we found some interesting things." As we opened the door to the room, I could see what the young man was referring to. Scattered on the floor were sheets, pillows, bed clothing and small white paper bindles as well as cigarette butts, roaches, and drug paraphernalia.

Subsequent investigation showed one of the girls had stolen a car in southern California and had driven it to San Jose. Along the way, she had helped herself to the credit cards in a purse left in the vehicle, charging about $1,500 worth of merchandise.

The next morning the girls were located at a downtown hotel, and both search and arrest warrants were obtained. The hotel manager told us his maid had checked earlier, reporting that someone was in the room in question, but that the door was locked and she didn't know who it was.

We decided to wait in an empty room next to the suspects'. A short time later the maid came in to report excitedly that the girl we wanted had just gotten off the elevator with three men and had gone into her room.

Sergeant Utts waited about five minutes then took the pass key and opened the suspects' door. "You're all under arrest for possession and transportation of drugs," he announced. The men turned pale and the two girls yelled about our violating their constitutional rights. It was obvious the three men knew nothing of the drug dealing, so they were cleared of those charges after questioning. While they were being interviewed in another suite, Sergeant Utts and I got busy searching the room. We found a hyp kit containing a spoon and two needles.

I was looking through a dresser drawer when I heard a voice say, "Okay, you're going to get it!" I looked around and one of the girls had a .38 levelled right at Ron Utts. At this point I decided I was in the wrong business! I then figured she was going to shoot somebody and it could very well be me! How I longed for the happy days back on a basketball floor!

I'd often seen scenes like this on television, but there was no play acting in this situation. I expected to hear a blast and see Ron fall, but the girl was talking to him. Then, suddenly, she pointed the gun directly at me, and, believe me, it looked more like a cannon than a little old .38! The switch in direction gave Ron the chance he needed and he was on her in a flash. He cracked her wrist and grabbed the weapon. It was all over in a matter of minutes—a fairly routine event for the seasoned detectives, but a shattering experience for me.

I later listened as the two girls, in their early twenties, were interrogated. I don't think my heart has ever gone out to two people more than it did to those two girls. They had come from good families and then got caught up in the drug scene. For four to five years they had engaged in prostitution to support their growing habit. Life had become a living hell from which they could see no escape.

Mr. Bowen went on several other raids which gave him opportunity to talk with young adults shooting heroin. He later transferred to a unit working on juvenile drug cases. It's one thing to read about young people in the drug scene and quite another to actually talk to the young people involved and learn some of the things they use to "turn on."

He talked with young people who had tried inhaling hair sprays from pressurized cans, Teflon (used to make pans stick-proof), and other dangerous inhalants. Some had tried mixing eyewash with roll-on deodorant and drinking it, while others ingeniously had tried bell peppers (by placing them outside under large glasses they believed the ultra violet rays of the sun would aid certain types of chemical reactions). Volatile chemicals—such as gasoline, glue, and paint thinner—produced for many youngsters an immediate, and dangerous, high.

Mr. Bowen recalls the first youngster he ever talked with in the drug scene. He asked her why she had become involved, and she replied, "I was really curious. I heard so much about marijuana that I had to try it. I enjoyed the feeling off of it, and later was told I would get a far bigger sensation from LSD so I went on to that."

Two of the main reasons teen-agers use drugs are *curiosity* and *peer group pressure*. And that pressure can be intense. "Everyone else is doing it" often is the only justification needed to try anything. A youngster wants more than anything else to be "in," accepted by the group, and if that group is using drugs it is next to impossible for an individual young person to stay away from it.

Experimentation is a key enticement. Many very intelligent students get carried away with the belief drugs will expand their minds and give them a better understanding of themselves. Or they feel if they drop some acid they will be able to solve a complicated problem, compose some beautiful poetry, or paint a lovely picture. But this creativity drugs supposedly offer is more illusion than fact. No one becomes more capable or competent in performing responsible tasks under the influence of hallucinogens. Inner turmoil and tension may be released but not in a way in which they can be effectively handled.

Rebellion is another reason students arrested offered for their drug use. Their frustrations with war, the establishment, evils in society, their parents— all were too big to be handled. And drugs offered a ready escape.

Hedonistically inclined young people many times get plain *pleasure* from using drugs. They know the warnings from ill-informed adults who say, "Drugs are no fun . . . you won't enjoy it," are often misleading. If a young person has no conscience and little sense of responsibility, drugs can appear very attractive indeed.

Consider Gail's comments in juvenile hall: "I used to run with a group of kids who were turning on. I thought I would never use drugs, but I started using a little marijuana and I 'enjoyed it. I finally decided, on a dare, to try some acid. I didn't think the marijuana was going to have a harmful effect on me so I figured LSD probably wouldn't either. I used to drop acid right after physical education class first period in the morning. I would hallucinate all day. Wow, it was great. It was very entertaining to see my English teacher go up to the board. I could stare at him and watch him grow long pointed ears and a beard. It was groovy."

It's fairly easy to get reasons why kids use drugs. But maybe you never know the truth after all. It can be difficult counseling and getting through to youngsters on drugs. There is no guarantee, either, that you can successfully help these young people unless (or until) there is a genuine change in their own philosophy, goals, view of themselves, and personality. But even that *can* happen, as later case histories will prove.

Mr. Bowen also spent some time with the Border Patrol and Customs agents at the United States-Mexican border, studying the drug inflow problem first hand.

One interesting investigation involved a young fellow in his early twenties who was using a lobster boat to bring marijuana up from Mexico for sale to contacts in San Francisco, New York, and Honolulu. The day of his arrest he had just shipped forty-seven kilos by air freight to New York.

Border inspectors have found marijuana under back seats of automobiles, in hubcaps, taped under fenders, behind the headlights, and, of course, stashed in the trunk. But some less obvious ways are used to hide some of the heavier drugs. People will swallow a balloon with a quantity of heroin. Then after nature takes its course, they get their heroin back! If the balloon should break in the digestive tract, the person would die quickly from an overdose of the drug. But the profits are so great many pushers consider such risks worthwhile. Other quantities of drugs have been hidden at the bottom of a dirty diaper pail. (It takes a very conscientious agent indeed to go fishing around in a pile of soiled diapers looking for narcotics!) One imaginative mother attempted to bring her illegal drugs across the border hidden in the bottle she was feeding her baby at the time she was stopped at the border.

But stopping drugs at the border is a very serious, and sometimes deadly, business.

Agents spend many lonely hours patrolling deserted land areas and waterways. A favorite smuggling technique, for example, is to bury marijuana among the catches on shrimp boats, then deep-freeze it along with the shrimp for shipment to the United States in refrigerated trucks.

Various Mexican family gangs have control of certain smuggling territories along the border and guard them jealously. These groups will pay several thousand dollars on a contract to murder an informer or agent. One agent today drives a souped-up Dodge formerly owned by an assassination squad sent to fulfill a contract. The agents got there first.

Agents depend heavily on informers (their "snitch" or "little finger") who ply a dangerous game. A number are slain each year. *Life* magazine reports one informer recently called an agent to finger half an ounce of heroin that was coming across the bridge hidden in the air filter of a car. When inspectors searched the filter they found a note inside, carefully addressed to the agent by name. "Dear Mr. Kilman," it read, "You have just lost your little finger."

The Haight-Ashbury scene changes all the time, but remains a constant source for the flow of drugs. From the district come large amounts of reds, yellows, and marijuana. It never seems to drop from the scene despite periodic clampdowns.

When Haight-Ashbury was at its height, idealistic flower children appeared to be building for themselves a novel place in contemporary American history. Young people would travel from all over the nation to be part of the scene, looking for excitement, adventure, a new way of living, and the great freedom they had vaguely heard the drug scene offered.

Mr. Bowen spent many days talking with kids on the streets. They were open and friendly. They would share their problems, explain why they were there, and talk about remaking society. And they were sincere in their aims. They would take Hack to their pads, where eight or ten people would live and sleep in the same room. They would share their food, most of which had been panhandled on the street. They would talk readily about free love and very little about the rising venereal disease rate such practices brought to the area. They even wore buttons saying, "Syphilis can be fun." And the kids were just as eager to share their drugs as they were their food and their bodies. To say they were shaking up their elders was only to compliment them. The only thing that mattered was to be willing to share and to "do your own thing."

Gradually the idealism of the streets gave way to con artists, thugs, exploiters, and hard-core drug pushers who made the young people, and the whole community, their victims. Peace and love are gone from the streets of the district today. All that remains is crime and violence.

When Mr. Bowen returned to his school district, it was with definite ideas on both teaching and counseling. The instruction would have to be fair, up-to-date, and meaningful.

New techniques, materials, and visual aids would have to be developed. Commenting on the films he had seen in drug education classes, one student told *Newsweek,* "The movies they show us about drugs are so stupid they're funny. They usually characterize the drug pusher as some greasy hoodlum who hangs around the football field looking sinister and luring kids. The reality is that the pusher is just another kid who happens to have some contacts— with dropouts, college kids, older people who can get the stuff."

The counseling would have to offer help and guidance, not merely threats and punishment. The young pushers would have to be dealt with, but with the realization that many of them, too, were often victims of greedy exploiters.

A close working relationship would have to be developed with the police, juvenile court, and counseling agencies. Parents would have to be informed. And the school staff would have to have positive guidelines of what to do in individual cases that came to their attention.

Counselors would have to be ready with facts and understanding when students came for help. They would also have to know their limitations. For example, they do *not* have privileged communication in keeping a law violation confidential if they should be asked by a legal authority for such information.

Guidelines would have to be set for administrators in dealing with individual students they found using drugs or who had been arrested. Several options were left open and the decisions made on an individual basis based on the student's involvement, history, and attitude.

One recommendation was to take the student involved with drugs back into his regular school program. If he had learned his lesson he might very well be a good influence on other students. We often get so wrapped up in thinking of possible bad influences teens have on each other, we tend to forget the opposite often is true.

Another choice was the use of the district continuation school, which offers a special program of academic work and guidance to students who, for a variety of reasons, cannot be kept in a regular school program. This continuation school can be most beneficial when a change of attitude is needed or when the situation is so serious the student should not immediately be returned to his regular classes. Continuation schools should *not* be used as a dumping ground to get rid of the problem by getting rid of the student. Every effort should be made to help the student at such a specialized school, and the goal should be the earliest possible return to regular school, taking into account all of the circumstances.

A third possibility is a transfer to another regular high school within the district when it is felt all that is needed is a change of crowd to reinforce what is basically a well-meaning, but involved, student.

The last alternative is expulsion. For this, action by the school board is necessary. It is used only as a last resort with youngsters who have been furnishing drugs, involving many other youngsters, and displaying an attitude where keeping him with the rest of the student body would be inviting more serious problems.

These procedures have worked well in practice, especially when applied carefully and on an individual basis. Other districts across the country have developed their own education-counseling programs. For example, John Imhof co-ordinates the program at Lynbrook High School, Lynbrook, New York, and Arthur Suddjian, who formerly headed the schools program in Fresno, has been made coordinator of the California State Office of Narcotics and Drug Abuse.

Mr. Bowen worked with one young girl heavily involved with drugs who had been found out by her parents, placed in juvenile hall with the evidence, and later returned to school. Because of the pressure placed on the girl by other students, her parents wanted her put in another school, and it was agreed this might be very wise. In her new school, she was able to break with the drug crowd, quickly became active in school affairs, regained sight of her aims and goals, and seems very happy in her new surroundings.

She has found a way to be a cure, not a cause; part of the solution instead of part of the problem. For a school district, that spells success.

"Just leave me alone! I'm going to do what I want to do!" How many times parents have heard those statements. Rich's folks heard them too, from their son, a senior in high school. He had used some pot. His parents knew it and became even more concerned as his grades dropped along with his interest in sports and other activities. They tried to get counseling for him, but Rich's attitude was, "Thanks, but no thanks." Then they began to suspect he might be trying other drugs.

That was it! They brought their suspicions and evidence to Mr. Bowen. After discussing it carefully, the parents made a very difficult decision. They requested their boy be placed in juvenile hall for drug use and as being beyond their control.

As might be expected, the person least enthusiastic about the arrangement was Rich. In fact, he was bitter, resentful, and angry—and he let everyone know it. But gradually he calmed down and began to listen as Mr. Bowen and the court staff told him that what had been done was designed to help him, not hurt him. Besides, home started looking like a pretty nice place compared to a juvie unit. If the price of getting back home was to lay off drugs, he just might agree to it.

He was released a few days later, and his school principal agreed, on Mr. Bowen's recommendation, to accept the boy back in his regular classes while he was receiving regular counseling help. Perhaps the problem was solved.

No such luck. Before long Rich was back to his crowd and his joints, and the principal found out about it. The boy was meek and scared now at the conference with his principal, dean, and parents, and it was decided to give him another chance.

The follow-up counseling work was intensified, but the results were not satisfactory despite the best efforts of school, parents, pastor, and probation officer.

How far should a school go in giving a youngster repeated chances? The principal, who was the key to this situation, was far more willing to help than most people would have been, and slowly the effort paid off.

Rich made it through high school and is now working, going to church regularly, and attending college. He's decided his career and his future are worth more than the risks from involvement with the drug scene.

We got a phone call from Rich the other day. "Look, there's this girl I know real well in high school," he said. "I think she's getting messed up on reds. I tried to tell her that's no way to go. Do you think you guys could give her some help. . . ."

He'll probably make it.

THE COURTS
ARE THEY HELPING ?

One out of every six boys and one of every twenty-four girls between the ages of ten and seventeen will be referred to juvenile court on delinquency charges. Of those whose cases are heard each year, roughly one in ten will be committed to a correctional institution. This is the estimate of the Children's Bureau of the Department of Health, Education, and Welfare. As drug abuse is becoming a growing problem among youth, more and more referrals are being made to the courts and institutions for offenses related to marijuana, restricted or dangerous drugs, and narcotics.

Details on the procedure at juvenile court and the operation of youth correctional facilities are given in Mr. McLean's book, *We're Holding Your Son*, but it will be helpful to update that material and apply it particularly to youngsters involved with drugs.

Perhaps few messages can strike more fear and dread in a parent's mind than that given in a late night call from the police: "We've picked up your youngster. Will you please come down to the station?" The grief is compounded if the parent is learning for the first time that the son or daughter is on drugs.

Suppose this happens to you. After determining it is your child who is in custody—that no mistake has been made despite your stunned response, "It can't be *my* son (or daughter)"—and after your sudden burst of emotion has subsided, what do you do next?

First, talk with the probation officer. Do this whether your youngster is released to you at the station that night or is held in custody. It may mean waiting until the next day. This officer can advise you of the charges filed, the circumstances of the arrest, and give you the general direction your particular juvenile court will go in reaching a disposition. He will also allow you to see your youngster privately so you can learn firsthand your child's version. Keep in mind a youth may be too upset or afraid to be fully honest at this point. Above all, don't go to pieces yourself, and don't say, "How could you do this to us after all we've done for you?" There will be plenty of time later for a full and frank family discussion.

At this time you should be aware of certain rights your youngster has. Many juvenile courts across the nation do not operate by these guidelines but the United States Supreme Court has carefully spelled them out:

1. The right to an attorney, and to have one appointed at government expense if the youngster or his family cannot afford one.

2. The right to specific notice of the charges against him.

3. The opportunity to confront any witnesses called to prove a charge against him and to cross-examine those witnesses, as well as to have the assistance of the court to compel the presence of any witnesses in his favor.

4. The privilege to remain silent.

5. The right of appeal to a higher court of review.

6. The right to a transcript or record of the proceedings.

That first one is most important. Should you have any question about your youngster's guilt, or should you feel the disposition being proposed by the probation department is not fair or otherwise in your child's best interests, then by all means insist on the services of an attorney.

A detailed and interesting presentation of a teen-ager's legal rights is provided in John Paul Hanna's book, *Teen-agers and the Law,* published by John Wiley and Sons.

"If my youngster is not released right away, where will he be held until his court hearing?" That's a good question. A total of 2,800 counties, over 90 percent, in the United States have only jails or jail-like holding facilities for youngsters in trouble with the law, and these facilities house more than 100,000 children every year, according to the National Council on Crime and Delinquency (NCCD).

In Los Angeles, the juvenile hall processes some two thousand children a month. There is room for 400 boys and 162 girls, but the day we visited there were more than a thousand youngsters in residence, with the overflow sleeping on mats on the floor. Audy House serves as Chicago's detention center, while 175 boys, ages sixteen to eighteen, are housed in the dismal conditions of the Philadelphia House of Correction. In many communities across the nation, they will simply be put in city or county jails, most of which are not considered acceptable by the Federal Bureau of Prisons for even temporary housing of adult federal felons!

If your community has an adequate juvenile detention facility—and slowly their number is increasing—you can rest easy.

In the San Jose, California, area, youngsters requiring detention will be housed in the Santa Clara County Juvenile Center—a beautiful, spacious building in the heart of the city, offering clean, comfortable facilities, age and maturity level segregation, good food, and a well-trained and dedicated supervision staff. This type of facility is no accident, nor did its staff and program come about overnight. It is the result of the earnest efforts of Chief Probation Officer Robert Nino and the response of an enlightened community. In this kind of facility a short period of detention often can bring about a meaningful reevaluation and appreciation for his home from a delinquent youngster, especially if the youngster comes from a fairly good home that he has taken for granted.

During his stay at the juvenile center, the youngster will be interviewed by a probation officer, have some school classes, get outdoors for recreation, and meet the two fine full-time chaplains, Brother Wellington J. Stanislaus, S. J., and Don Phillips.

When it is time to go to court, the first issue will be whether the petition charging the offense is true or not. Once that petition is admitted or sustained following the hearing of evidence, the judge will then read a background investigation report prepared by the probation department. It outlines the youngster's previous history of difficulties, home situation, school record, attitude, and finally a recommendation as to what the department feels the disposition should be. The judge also will hear from the attorney for the youngster, the youngster himself, and the parents before making his determination, which is usually—but certainly not always—what the department is requesting.

The procedure outlined here may be a far cry from practices in your community, but remember that each element of it is a right to which you are entitled. In some sections of the South, youngsters actually are sent to reform schools without their parents knowing it! A child may be picked up at night, jailed, taken before a judge in the morning, and hauled off to the reform school before lunch. There also are instances—we recall some in Washington state—where youngsters were sent to state institutions without ever having appeared in court.

The most difficult part of juvenile court hearings is determining what should be done with the youngster to best bring about his rehabilitation. Particularly in drug cases, the matter is not easily resolved. The matter of disposition is influenced by the philosophy of the judge and the probation department, the resources available, community feeling and pressure, and the home situation of the child.

One of the biggest weaknesses in most juvenile court dispositions is that the young person is not sufficiently impressed with the seriousness of his offense the first time around. If he were, he might not be back. But the thought that everybody is entitled to one mistake, that the youth seems repentant at the time, that his parents are concerned, and that his attorney is at hand all combine to bring about a quick release. Often there is no detention period, perhaps not a court hearing, and very little in the way of probation supervision. We've seen many young people who were handled this way get into further trouble. They then find the court quite severe, and say, "If only they'd been strict the first time." Hearings whenever possible, a short period of detention under the proper conditions, a firm probation plan, and careful supervision are needed to impress some youngsters who have never had limits placed on them in their lives.

The view that all first-timers should be released doesn't make much sense either. When certain youngsters appear in juvenile hall, it is obvious from their background, their offense, and their attitude that they will be back. But except for the most severe crimes, rarely will a juvenile court come to grips with the needs of these youngsters until a second or third offense.

On the other hand, there is a tendency to deal with all repeaters and those who have committed serious offenses (in the drug field, pushers are in this category) as needing out-of-home placement, generally in a correctional institution. This kind of disposition may be called for, but it may not be.

When there is a doubt, should not the youngster's home be given a chance again?

The law favors it. For example, consider section 502 of the California Welfare and Institutions Code (and similar provisions written into the laws of most other states): "The purpose of this chapter is to secure for each minor under the jurisdiction of the juvenile court such care and guidance, preferably in his own home, as will serve the spiritual, emotional, mental, and physical welfare of the minor and the best interests of the state; to preserve and strengthen the minor's family ties whenever possible, removing him from the custody of his parents only when his welfare or the safety and protection of the public cannot be adequately safeguarded without removal. . . . This chapter shall be liberally construed to carry out these purposes."

Alternative private placements are often not available, not adequate, or too expensive. Willing relatives in other communities—the greater the distance the better—often are asked to take a youngster, who may be almost a stranger to them. Calling such an arrangement strained is to flatter it extremely. Changing a boy's environment won't solve his problems. He may take them with him, and he can find disturbed kids with whom to associate in any community. Placement with relatives should be considered only when the youngster's home is plainly inadequate.

Institutionalizing a youngster simply because of a serious or repeated offense with no regard to the kind of person he is may be actually very detrimental to him. Charles Alexander of the Santa

Clara County Juvenile Rehabilitation Facility comments on the "prosocial offender" who often uses drugs or commits other serious offenses: "Most of these offenders really need no rehabilitative treatment at all. The problem with some of them is to get them out of the correctional cycle before they are harmed by contact with other offenders. . . . One study . . . in a reformatory . . . found the lowest recidivism rates among the members of this type who served the briefest possible sentences and who were isolated and not involved in therapy programs." (The report goes on to describe other types of offenders who definitely do need institutional treatment.)

Community resources often can be used to help these young people which, in the long run, will be more helpful than institutional treatment. Individual and group counseling, family services, private tutoring, church youth programs, recreational and social groups can all be utilized, and for far less than the $8,000 a year it often costs to lock a young person up.

Our juvenile court has a Special Supervision Unit where reduced caseloads, skillful staff, and full program combine to have a pronounced effect for good on some very delinquent youngsters. The only thing wrong with the project is it needs to be larger. Group discussions, a drug-abuse counseling group with teens and parents talking out their problems are additional facets of the court program.

But suppose institutional treatment *is* called for, then what?

Again the quality of treatment offered will vary

by community and state. A few facilities will be unbelievably good, most intolerably bad. But that shouldn't be surprising. A look at a few figures from the Department of Commerce will quickly show where Americans put their priorities. In a recent year, we spent $36.6 billion dollars on automobiles and parts. Another $14.5 billion went for alcoholic beverages; while $9.2 billion was spent on tobacco products. We even spent $2 billion a year on pets. Yet the total spent for 110,000 children locked in reform schools was only a fraction of that —an estimated $209 million according to the Department of Health, Education, and Welfare.

That is considerably less than the cost of a week of the Vietnam war, according to the *Christian Science Monitor,* which gathered the figures.

A boy may be sent to a correctional school like McLaren School in Oregon, Green Hill School in Washington, O. H. Close School in California, Lyman School in Massachusetts, Fairfield School in Ohio, the Camp Hill State Correctional Institution in Pennsylvania, the Iowa Training School at Eldora, or the Cheshire Reformatory in Connecticut.

The programs in the various institutions will vary. You'll find the *moral training program* with a stress on discipline and repressive confinement; the *vocational trainers* who feel the answer to juvenile ills is to teach Junior a trade; the *recreation* advocates who believe teaching a boy to play is teaching him to live with his fellow man; the *relaxed permissive* believers who feel a happy child is a well-adjusted child; the *school achievement* group who are convinced social adjustment can be brought about by teaching delinquents to read better; and the *diagnostic theorists* who left their parlor games of testing to determine why Junior blows pot. They are now all put together on a *treatment team,* supposedly working together and blending their various skills, but each more apt to be concerned about the importance of his own brand of magic.

Even the most enlightened counseling programs are not always effective in meeting the needs of teens on drugs. Institutions first isolate the youngster from the surroundings of his home, and then often imply he is mentally ill because of all sorts of traumatic experiences in his background which need to be carefully probed before he can be cured.

Are most of these youngsters mentally ill? Not according to Dr. William Glasser. Discussing deficiencies in the treatment of withdrawn youngsters, Dr. Glasser writes in *Schools without Failure:*

"They suffer and withdraw because they can't find the successful pathways to a successful identity. We wrongly label variations of this suffering and withdrawal 'mental illness.' Such people are not ill; nothing has happened to them that they can't remedy themselves. Illness implies that a person has been attacked by a bacteria, toxin, or chemical imbalance over which he has no control. In helping children, we must work to make them understand that *they are responsible* for fulfilling their needs, for behaving so that they can gain a successful identity. No one can do it for them. If they continue to choose pathways that lead to failure, that diminish their self-worth, that are without love, they will continue to suffer and continue to react with delinquency or withdrawal."

Dr. Glasser believes strongly that young people who are acting irresponsibly need strong and emotional involvement with those who can make responsible decisions.

Putting this principle to work in a confinement setting with youngsters who have been on drugs is not easy, but our Santa Clara County juvenile department at its rehabilitation facilities is trying. The two boys ranches, located at Morgan Hill, must be ranked among the finest such facilities in the nation. For a youngster and his family who need their services, the ranches offer tremendous assistance. The emphasis is strongly on individual and group counseling led by a generally well-qualified staff. Recreation, education, and home consultations are all built around the counseling center of the program.

And a spiritual ministry for these young people who have used drugs is a must. "For these young people," comments Charles Alexander in a treatment evaluation, "there is no effective answer that leaves out a spiritual influence. Threat of confinement in the future, even good counseling, often falls short of the desired goal. That's because there is an emptiness in most of these lives. That particular goal can be met only with a spiritual answer. I know that a youth who meets the Lord in a genuine experience and is exposed to a new pattern of living and friendships will come out with his life changed. That is why the work of our chaplains and the assistance of Campus Life is an important part of our over-all treatment both in confinement and upon release back home."

And he can point to boys like Ray and Randy as examples. Ray came to the ranch because of his deep involvement with drugs—before he left he was president of the ranch student council and is now active in our Drug Abuse Information school programs while he goes on to college. His friend Randy, with a long history of drug use and school problems, also found the help he needed in the ranch program and through his personal spiritual commitment. No one, including Randy, really expected him to change when he was busted. But he has, and is doing well.

Our law enforcement agencies and courts have an important, and admittedly difficult, responsibility in meeting the growing crime problem in general, and the youth drug abuse problem in particular.

The agencies' success never will be enhanced if they are taken up with the thought that punishment alone will ease the crisis. It certainly won't until it is meted out to the upper echelon of the underworld leaders exploiting the weaknesses of youth—those who often escape detection and arrest. And it won't until the institutions to which we send young people and adults are more than training grounds for newer and more advanced crimes.

Punishment rarely deters the person threatened with it, let alone anyone else. His associates generally feel the person caught was only stupid or unfortunate. Nobody ever does anything wrong with the thought of being caught. At least such instances are rare. If punishment is designed as a deterrent, we'd better take a long, second look at its dismal record of failure before we continue to advocate it. We had also better learn that when it comes to the administration of justice, what is best for the individual is, in the long run, in the best interests of society.

Of late we have been overly concerned in our country with Supreme Court rulings that have done nothing more than extend the safeguards and guarantees of freedom in the Constitution and the Bill of Rights to every citizen. Listening to the violent outcries against the court gives cause to wonder whether some Americans *really* believe in the documents that safeguard our independence and freedom. Of course these rulings limit police activity. They were intended to, as was the Bill of Rights. It might be good to remember there are places in this world where guarantees of freedom are not worth the paper they are written on and where police have an absolutely free hand. Few of us would want to live there.

Our police departments *do* need help in the form of better training, better equipment, larger staffs, and increased salaries. They certainly don't need the kind of restriction that, for example, keeps them from searching the premises when they arrest a suspect—a particularly unfortunate limitation in narcotics cases. Nor do they need sensational journalists using headlines on brutality to play up every complaint against officers.

Juvenile courts should not threaten young people with dire consequences and institutional confinement if they commit further violations, only to turn around later and tell youngsters who are actually committed it is being done for their own good, not as punishment. The hypocrisy of such an approach is inescapable.

Above all, our law enforcement agencies and courts need the support of the public, which goes far beyond putting a bumper sticker on our cars and urging strict enforcement of the laws with which we happen to agree. It involves enlightened interest and knowledge. This takes time. It takes our willingness to offer assistance in an emergency, to give evidence in court, to serve on juries without dodging that responsibility, and to support with our tax dollars the kinds of programs that build adequate police, probation, and rehabilitation departments.

In many communities, confusion as to direction and eager—but uninformed—enthusiasm seem to mark the efforts of numerous groups of concerned, scared parents worried about the drug problem. Their efforts are best channeled into support for educational and counseling programs and urging their lawmakers, on both state and federal levels, to supply the programs and the funds to wage an all-out war on drug sellers while at the same time supplying guidance and counselors for teen-agers tragically involved.

And for the company of committed spiritual believers, the youth drug problem represents a great need and challenge to kindly, patiently, and faithfully point those in need to the One who said, "I am come to bring them life, and far more life than before." If the young doper can grasp that message, it can become for him the greatest Good News he will ever hear! But let us not be sidetracked into pressing a set religious formula, an organization, or a catalog of theological truths as a substitute. Only a personal encounter with the Son of God can transform a life.

One thing is certain. We cannot settle for the insipid style of so much contemporary religious program that has caused many young people to doubt the validity of the church as a realistic influence in their lives. Only a penetrating Gospel message presented in a contemporary style by concerned people can meet the need. The alternative is for the church to be passed by.

Even worse than religious mishandling, we dare not settle for simply wringing our hands as we decry the evils and trends of our day. Surely we aren't naive enough to think our world would go in any other direction than that of which the Bible warns. Hopefully we will not stoop to shouting for punitive revenge on those who have erred, when we could work for intelligent redirection and a sense of worth and responsibility in broken lives. To do less than this is to miss the mark and a great opportunity for service. Worse, it is unworthy of Him who gave His life for a lost world, and therefore, unworthy of us who are His followers.

DRUGS CAN KILL!

The sudden outburst of applause in the Leland High School, San Jose, gym was for a guy deeply involved in a tragedy.

Students don't usually sit in silence for an hour. But the subject was dope, and they were transfixed. At times faces winced. Now and then there was a gasp, the clamp of a hand across a mouth. But at the end, hands clapped in appreciation.

Drew, only a few years older than the miniskirted girls and the lean guys in his audience, told how he had become interested in drugs as a senior in high school when national magazines were playing up psychedelic drugs and Timothy Leary was advocating the use of LSD. A friend of his older brother had invited him to try some marijuana.

"All your friends are doing it, so soon you are forced into it yourself," Drew told the kids. "I found that through my prolonged use of marijuana, I lost my ambition. My sense of values changed. After you smoke marijuana awhile you want to become more stoned, so you go on to other drugs."

After high school, he told them, he went to Europe for a year. He worked hard and started popping pills, working up to fifteen a day.

"When I came home I went back to some of my old friends who had been using grass," he said. "In one month I started methedrine. You can sniff it, take it orally, skin pop it, or mainline.

"First you get a rocking sensation, called a flash. Then an ether feeling. You become hyperactive and want to move about.

"You build up. The first time I fixed for a dollar's worth. At the end I was fixing eight times a day at $40 or $50 per day."

Drew financed his habit at first with money supplied unknowingly by his parents. (He exhausted a $10,000 trust fund, from drug use and medical treatment he later needed.)

"Eventually, I went to stealing—which is inevitable if you go onto hard drugs.

"I've taken acid seventy-five to a hundred times and never had a bad trip," Drew explained to his audience. "But many of my friends are in Agnews (state mental hospital), or they are walking vegetables."

Drew told of his efforts to kick the habit.

"I've had three psychiatrists. The first one used drugs, too. I was in worse shape with him.

"It is common among methedrine users to become attracted to needles, to become needle freaks. You will shoot anything into you just to feel the needle. I've even shot wine."

Drew said he became a needle freak, then continued:

"If you shoot a lot of drugs, it is almost inevitable you will catch serum hepatitis. It comes from using dirty needles and attacks your liver.

"At first you play doctor and try to keep the needle sterile. Then as time goes on, you don't care. Once I was in a restroom with a friend and we dropped a needle in the toilet bowl. We just fished it out and used it."

Drew developed hepatitis. A doctor told him if he didn't change his mode of living, he would be dead in one year.

But the real sense of horror washed over the students' faces as they listened to Drew tell about what happened to his sixteen-year-old girl friend after she took a fix of cocaine. He had met her about six months before, "through another friend, a real hard user. The first time I met her she was shooting methedrine."

However, she had quit methedrine two weeks before the night in question. "She got bored easily," Drew said. He and the young girl were at an acquaintance's home with a half-dozen others and "she had taken some cocaine." Three young people were in the room—Drew, his girl friend, and David. She got some more cocaine, went in the other room, mixed and shot the drug herself. She immediately went into convulsions.

Drew rushed her to the hospital, but she died on the way. Deaths of young drug users are, unfortunately, not rare. New York City alone averages one a day.

In six weeks, Drew told his story to some 25,000 students, explaining his own drug use and the reason he was standing trial for murder (he allegedly handed his girl friend the cocaine that was the final, lethal dose). After the assemblies, students would pepper him with questions until he would have to leave for the next appointment. Neatly attired, calm and casual, Drew made a profound impression. Civic clubs, churches, radio and TV requested appearances.

His hearers could be excused for wondering whether the pleasant young man standing beside Mr. McLean had *really* been deeply involved in the drug scene. He looked more like a quiet college student (which he was at that point) than a junkie.

How could he have changed so drastically? Who ever heard of a young man out on bail awaiting a murder charge being warmly welcomed by school administrators and community leaders?

Drew had come up a long, difficult route from the bottom of the drug ladder. We met him shortly after he was booked into the county jail. He was a physical and mental wreck from the drugs and the anxiety about the second-degree murder charges and the discomforts of maximum security.

Before long, his family had arranged bail, and the work of his capable young attorney, John Griffiths, reassured him somewhat. But getting released from custody to await trial didn't solve his problems. In fact, in a way it added to them, for now he was pressured simply to run away and escape it all. Friends in the drug scene were eager to welcome him back. There was the thought he should "just o.d. (overdose) and end it all." There were deep feelings for his girl friend and what had happened to her.

Despite the pressures, something in Drew wouldn't allow him to "o.d." or to cop out—something that said, "I'm going to lick these things and come out on top."

But how? Where do you turn to rebuild a broken life? Friends, counselors, teachers, employers, activities—all can help, but none can give you peace about living when the past is still there. The means "to come out on top" eluded him, and the pressures almost made him give up the search.

We spent many long hours talking about all this. We pointed out that only God could perform the spiritual heart surgery—delicate work for the hands of only one Specialist.

One day, quietly and alone, Drew opened the door of his life to the Lord. Not that his problems, discouragements, and battles weren't still there. They were. But now Drew had a tremendous resource within him with which to face those issues. He comments now, "I accepted the Lord into my life. This is the only way I've been able to lick drugs."

His confidence increased. He was able to get a regular job and return to college classes and even earn good grades—none of which he had been able to do since starting out on drugs.

And as he got acquainted with the Campus Life staff and our high school activities, he became increasingly concerned about the drug-abuse problem among students, most of whom had read about his case in the press. By frankly discussing drugs he just might be able to influence some of them to think twice before getting deeply and perhaps tragically involved.

Of course, his talks could be misunderstood. There would be those who would think it was sensationalizing or trying to influence the outcome of the forthcoming trial. Actually, far from being pleased, Drew's attorney was concerned that the talks would jeopardize the case. But well aware of the risks, Drew went ahead anyway.

After some delays, his case was set for trial but not until after a court order had been sought to stop Drew's speaking and to hold up publication of *We're Holding Your Son* which discussed Drew's case and to which he had written the foreword. The matter was resolved in court by our agreeing not to discuss the case in any talks and to hold up local distribution of the book until after the trial.

The day a jury was to be selected, Drew and David entered guilty pleas to a reduced charge of involuntary manslaughter. Drew was given a three-year suspended sentence on condition he serve eight months in the county jail, while David was given an indefinite commitment to the California Youth Authority.

What of Drew's future? He would like to complete his education and study for the ministry, specializing in youth counseling and drug abuse work.

Of course, not everyone who has used drugs would feel as Drew does, perhaps because few of them have had as deep an involvement or as tragic a result. How does the more casual college student feel, one still using drugs? We got a rare opportunity to gain that perspective from a letter written to KLIV radio's Scott St. James after Scott had discussed drugs on his program. Here are some of the highlights:

"I have been involved in the illicit drug scene for about four years. I am not freaked out and I have never been arrested. I admit a stoned person has some erratic behavior. He laughs at things that may not be funny, he eats sweets like a hog, he feels lazy, and he is not apt to participate in any activity that requires a great physical effort. Work is also a drag. The only real consequences I've noted from heavy pot users is that they may act more lazy than usual. I do know that a lot of psychological problems, such as the so-called generation gap, family troubles, etc., can lead a person to really enjoy pot and therefore become a steady user. Among mentally well-adjusted persons there is no dependence on the weed, and there are no withdrawal symptoms among persons who abruptly stop using the weed.

"If a person is bold enough to try the illegal drug marijuana, and he sees it isn't really hurting him like all the papers say, he may be likely to try other drugs such as LSD, THC, etc. if the occasion arises. However, I know many people who are users of pot but who will never touch LSD, mescaline, etc. under any conditions.

"LSD produces hallucinations and exaggerates the senses. It is ingested into the system, and produces about a five-hour trip. Ordered color patterns in the vision, wavy and blurry eyesight, and a mushy sense of touch characterize the symptoms of LSD. Some trips are weak, some are strong. Some are pleasant, some are nightmares.

"In my own experiments (which are illegal) I have found that continued use of LSD does cause some psychological changes. The heavy acid user tends to pull away from social norms more than just a pot user. An acid freak seems to have a loss of initiative, and thinks that the best things in life are free. It puts the mind in a different perspective, and it makes it hard to equate with normal human standards. In other words, an acid head may be what people call a dropout from society.

"Personally, I feel that acid can be very nice for some people, but it has obvious harmful effects. You can wreck your mind or kill yourself with acid.

"Mescaline also causes hallucinations, a high like very weak acid, and you see more vivid colors. The ill effects are much less than with acid.

"Most of the so-called THC on the market is really a mixture of monkey tranquilizers, barbiturates, laxatives, etc. But apparently the majority of people who buy acid and mescaline either get what they wanted or they get burned. I feel if my friends want to use drugs, that is their concern. I use acid and mescaline very infrequently. I don't like to get that high very often. I have had only one trip on psilocybin, and it is too hard to obtain. The trip was good, similar to other hallucinogens, as I mentioned before. STP also is a hallucinogen. In my opinion it is the most powerful of all. An STP trip lasts at least sixteen hours, and it is strong. I tried STP accidentally, and all I can say is, never again. An STP user's mind deteriorates rapidly with every dose. Most of the zombies in the hippie cult have probably been destroyed by STP, because acid and mescaline are not that powerful, in my experience. I have no love for STP. If I ever come across any, I'll destroy it. The consequences of its use are just too rough.

"As for opium, heroin, and speed . . . well, they're deadly. I have never used heroin, but I have used opium. It was pleasant, but I will never repeat using it. It's too dangerous and harmful, as is heroin. Speed is the most pleasant of all the drugs I have used, and it is habit forming. I can see why so many people like it, but it is very dangerous. Many lives and minds have been destroyed by speed.

"All drugs have sociological effects, too. I am a felon, although I have never been arrested. I have experimented on myself and with others, and all these experiments were illegal. My instructor at college informed me they were illegal, but he did not refuse to accept my work. I feel I haven't harmed myself by using these drugs any more than a Friday-night drinker harms himself.

"One can easily die from reds, and I say, let them alone. I have used reds. I don't like them. They produce a drug intoxication that is not at all appealing. It is just too abnormal to be pleasurable to me.

"In conclusion, Scott, I feel that some drugs are good, some are hazardous, and some are deadly. I am not saying that I love drugs, and I am not saying that I dislike them. I think one should decide for himself if he wants to alter his consciousness or not, as long as he is not a hazard to others. The next generation may see some drastic changes, or it all may pass into extreme police and government controls. Only time will tell.

"For obvious reasons, I must remain as just plain 'Jim,' as I am a felon and I do not wish to have the word out. It's hot enough as it is.

"Yours truly for peace, Jim."

"PUSHING SOMETHING NEW"

In the desperate world of the dopers, where narcotics officers quickly become known to many of the pushers and junkies, most arrests can be made only by using such military devices as informers, or spies, camouflage, and patient surveillance from long distances. Police, often understaffed and overworked, like most other enforcement agencies, have time on their side. If they can lie in wait from dusk until dawn without breaking their strict discipline, or have an agent penetrate a circle of pushers, they can make their bust. Sooner or later the peddler has to sell.

And now these same tactics have been moved to the campus level to meet the growing threat of teenagers victimized by the drug traffic.

The head coach was irked, so, while the rest of the team drilled their routines, he motioned Bill over to the side. "Look," he growled, "last year you were really a clean kid. What in the world has happened to you? I don't like all this long hair and surly attitude. If you're gonna play on my team, at least get a haircut."

Bill looked down, made a squeak on the gym floor with his shoe, and muttered something that the coach didn't catch. The lecture was over, he guessed, so he moved back into the practice.

Next day, Bill had obviously not been to a barber. During PE, he was swimming with his class when the phone rang, requesting him to show up right away in the head coach's office. When he arrived, three other coaches also were present, ready to add to the comments whenever their leader needed a rest.

"Bill, we're getting sick and tired of your actions around here, not only in sports but in class as well. I told you yesterday to get a haircut, and you didn't even hear me. You're not only putting yourself down, you're also putting down your team and your school. Last year you were an all-American kid. This year you act and look like a Hell's Angel!"

It didn't really matter which of the four was speaking. They all said the same things.

Again Bill acted impatient with the whole scene, snarled back once in awhile, and got out as soon as he could. Once beyond the door, he fingered the sideburns an inch below his ear and smiled to himself. He also wondered how many more of these sessions he could take without really messing everything up. For Bill was dressing, talking and acting like one of the "dopers" at his San Jose, California, high school because he was one of the teen agents who occasionally make some outstanding "buys" for the local police! And not even his teachers knew it.

Bill had to play his part carefully—to be eager for contacts to buy around campus, but not too eager. He had to keep his ears open and his mouth shut.

He had to be shaggy in appearance, and somewhat radical in his views, especially where they related to drugs. The only school official who knew of his role was the principal, but he couldn't risk the whole operation by stepping in when teachers, coaches and counselors complained about Bill's "going down hill." It was a narrow line for him to walk between playing the role and not flunking or getting kicked out.

Bill acted his part almost too well in several of his classes. A biology teacher flunked him. Even the protests of Bill's dad couldn't change his mind. Bill's drafting grade went from a B first semester to a D second semester, because some in the class were members of the drug crowd, and Bill had to play the role especially heavy there, sometimes acting sleepy as if on "reds" (seconal tablets).

But this was a small price when compared to the dangers of drug abuse, which is what motivated Bill to take his curious job in the first place. Months before, a friend had offered him some reds at a party, and he took several—enough to make him sick. Far from a pleasant sensation, he experienced nothing but nausea and upset; so much so he had a friend take him home and he went right to bed. His parents were out when he arrived, so he could easily have slept off the effects with no one the wiser. But he didn't, and therein the stage was set for an unusual police investigation that ended up making headlines.

A high school boy like Bill trying drugs is not unique. In California alone, thirty-three hundred teenagers a month are arrested on drug charges as a new menace rolls into high gear. Bill lives in San Jose, the principal city of the Santa Clara Valley. It's an affluent area with few slums. The largest minority group is the 20 percent Chicano population; blacks account for about 1 percent. The militant turmoil of racial unrest in Oakland and the college demonstrations at San Francisco State or the University of California at Berkeley make local headlines but are really far removed from the daily routine in the valley. There are seventy-five thousand students attending fifty-three county high schools— the vast majority of them as well off, if not more so, than most American teens. Their problems are boredom, intellectual unrest, and social concern rather than personal needs, and many of them have become ripe targets for, and later active participants in, a growing drug abuse problem that concerns parents, police, courts, and even teens themselves.

Bill, a senior, could pass for a typical high school fellow—well-built, goodlooking, and a basketball player. He tried the reds out of curiosity and because "all the guys are doing it"—standard excuses.

After his unpleasant evening, Bill talked over the situation with his parents. He told his folks how freely reds and other drugs were available. Suppliers on the high school campus often would give drugs to underclassmen and, once an appetite had been cultivated, sell to their unknowledgeable victims at highly-inflated prices. Later that morning, Bill talked with school officials.

The suggestion was made that Bill become an agent for the police. At this point we met Bill and realized, with him, that student users probably could be helped by a counseling program, but suppliers had to be stopped first by being arrested—then maybe they'd listen.

Bill had a real concern not only to see the drug scene busted open, but to help the students who were involved. Why? Because the previous summer he had attended a summer camp sponsored by Young Life that had had a pronounced spiritual impact on his own way of living. He was concerned and, more important, willing to be involved. He would make a good agent.

There are a number of agents, usually older than teen-agers—special employees they are called—working with Lieutenant Stan Hardman and the Narcotics Unit of the San Jose police. They are skillful at playing their part and fully realize the dangers involved. They know, for example, their role may be exposed if a supplier pleads not guilty and they are brought into court to testify. But that doesn't happen often. The evidence gathered with witnesses, hidden recorders and cameras, when shown to a suspect, usually produces an admission to the charge. Several young agents are former users and pushers; at least one had been committed to a juvenile institution on narcotics charges. Another volunteered when his girl friend got turned on from speed with near-disastrous results. The teen-agers usually work in company with an older agent who is a young police officer acting as a pusher or junkie.

Of course the drug crowd likes to spot an agent and ruin his effectiveness, if not worse. One trusted user was asked, "Don't you think Joe is a stooly for the fuzz?" "Don't be stupid," was the reply, "I turn on with the guy. He's no more cop than I am." That ended the matter. What was said had been the truth, however. *Both* fellows were agents! At another campus, druggers staged a campaign to give some supposed narcs a bad time. The kids being singled out for the bad time weren't agents, but the boy leading the campaign was! Girls can be very helpful as informants, too. It seems pushers will trust anybody introduced to them by a girl they like, which has been the undoing of more than one big-time pusher.

For a teen-ager to play the role of a serious drugger, with appearance and attitude to match, takes some practice. It involves risks, and takes a lot of time. Parental consent is required, and teen employees are carefully told that under no condition are they ever to use drugs. There are several reasons for that last prohibition. One is that their use of drugs with a suspect would seriously damage the presentation of the case in court.

One situation Bill worked on involved the operator of a small grocery store who encouraged junior high age youngsters to steal radios, small recorders, and car parts. He paid for the merchandise with drugs. It was a distinct pleasure to put him out of business. While many operations went smoothly enough, working on cases among the high school students did present some problems.

An unexpected complication arose when one of Bill's buddies became concerned about Bill's involvement and threatened to either report Bill to the authorities or work over anyone who sold to him. As the friend was a wrestler, his was no idle boast!

Clearly something had to be done, and it was decided he could be trusted to know about the operation. When he was told Bill was working for the police, the friend was stunned, amazed, delighted—and then intrigued. He offered to be of assistance and once again the operation was on course.

Another teen agent called one night in near panic. While setting up some buys, he made a purchase from his cousin. These boys and their families were close friends, and our man had no knowledge his cousin was dealing until he found him with a known pusher and a sale was made. "I never knew this would happen," the young agent said, "but maybe it's best for it to happen now before he's in deeper. But please try to get him on the right road when he's busted." We agreed to try . . . and did.

The buys usually are carefully set up. In these investigations, Sergeants Dalton Rolen and Arnold Bertotti, and undercover police officer Richard Mazzone, would most often make the actual buys along with a special employee. The buys would be observed, if possible, by the sergeants and photographed as well as recorded to make a thorough evidence package for either the grand jury, court trial, or juvenile court hearing. The arrest may or may not be immediate. The case may rest awhile to allow a particular employee to make a series of buys before his effectiveness is ended by a string of arrests. Bill's series, involving several agents and undercover police officers, resulted in thirty-eight arrests, half of them juvenile pushers. Thousands of bennies, hundreds of reds, and a few kilos of marijuana were obtained at the time of the arrests.

At one home, the young suspect wasn't there, but two friends were—and they sold to the police. On a second try to catch the boy, some drugs were obtained from the suspect's mother! All three were later arrested along with the original suspect. As much as possible, there is a liaison between local police departments, the sheriff, and state and federal agencies in working drug cases.

The teen-agers arrested will go to juvenile court, and those charged with furnishing drugs will, in most instances, find the juvenile department recommending placement in either a public or private institution. Those with minor involvements and no previous history probably will go home under probationary supervision. Chief Probation Officer Robert Nino, Assistant Chief Richard Bothman, and their staff are doing a most effective job in helping youngsters caught up in the drug scene. They work closely with parents, schools, and counseling services to help redirect teen-agers involved.

The adults appear before the Criminal Division of the Superior Court, which has adhered to a rigid policy of jailing drug furnishers, a position which finds much support in the community.

One young man fled the state following his release from juvenile hall to await further hearing, but later returned and surrendered himself. His case was transferred to superior court but dismissed for lack of evidence. Another youth disputed the petition on furnishing marijuana on the grounds of entrapment —stating the idea of the sale was not really his, but Bill's acting for the police—and so it was necessary for Bill to appear in court, explain his role, and the circumstances under which the sale had been made. The judge sustained the petition as requested by the probation department.

But do any of these young people *really* learn from the experience, and change? Yes, they do.

There's Ken—a thin, nervous sixteen-year-old high school junior with long, blond hair and a two-year history of using and selling a variety of drugs. Emotion and thought competed for expression as he talked.

"Yes, I was bitter when I was busted. I knew it meant I'd probably go to the ranch, and all I could think of was hating those dirty cops and the lousy finks who helped them. But then I figured they couldn't have busted me if I wasn't doing it. And my P.O. (Probation Officer), Mr. Neary, he really wanted to help me but I wouldn't let him. I lied to him, and he knew it. I was a wise guy at school and wore out my welcome there . . .

"I wasn't raised that way. I'm mad at myself. I used to live in Boston, and I had a good time . . . none of this drug stuff. We were a happy family. Then I come out here and it's all bad news . . . drugs . . . and I'm in the middle of it. Now I guess even the guys where I used to live turn on, too. No matter what they do to me, I really want it to end. I'm through with this kind of stuff."

There's something about this boy that makes you believe him. Tears aren't going to get him out of an institution, and he knows it. He commented:

"If they let me out next week, next month, or not until next year, I want to stay clean. I'm not going back to dope."

And there's Pat, who wrote the foreword to this book. Pat is much like Bill—sharp, goodlooking, fine potential—but Pat was on the opposite side, a supplier. In custody, he recognized what he was doing to himself and his future, and also to his deeply concerned parents. He asked for help, emphasized his disillusionment with drugs, and has eagerly joined one of our drug abuse program teams. At his hearing, there was a letter of recommendation to the judge from Bill. The judge decided to keep Pat on juvenile status instead of sending him to adult court and granted probation—a break Pat may not really deserve, but which he most surely appreciates.

Many of these fellows find the support they need to redirect their lives at our Campus Life high school clubs and Youth for Christ Saturday night programs —an activity stressing the need for physical, mental, social, and spiritual balance in the life of teens. A spiritual commitment, filling a void in a way drugs never could, often gives them a whole new basis for living.

It hasn't been easy for Bill since the case broke. There have been two shots fired at him, he's been run off the road several times by carloads of hooligans, and a small explosive dented the trunk of his car one night. But Bill can take care of himself, and he is no coward. He saw a job that needed to be done and did it. He plans a career in law enforcement.

There was no money involved in the service he rendered. Bill is just a guy concerned that some kids get on the right track before their lives are ruined by drugs, a chain too weak to be felt until it's too strong to be broken.

The role of police working with young people need not be confined simply to investigation and arrest. Law enforcement agencies are becoming increasingly aware of their role in prevention.

"A considerable number of communities have made definite progress toward giving sharper definition to what police service for juveniles should be and how this should be carried out," comments Edward Eldefonso in his textbook for law enforcement training classes.[1] "To summarize some of these local developments, many police departments are now giving greater attention to training their officers in those modern concepts of law enforcement that emphasize protection, treatment, and rehabilitation of the child. In many places, officers have been appointed to work especially with children. In a considerable number of communities, special units or divisions have been established to carry on the work with juveniles. Special procedures have likewise been devised that are aimed at contributing to rehabilitation, and, at the same time, sparing the juvenile wrong-doer the public exposure and shame so often visited upon the adult. Finally, in those communities that have given particular attention to the problem of young people, the relation of the police to other community agencies has been strengthened and clarified, so that the police have a better understanding of what can and should be done for children through the use of other resources in the community."

---

[1] Edward Eldefonso, *Law Enforcement and the Youthful Offender* (New York: John Wiley & Sons, Inc., 1967).

Sometimes, stopping a young pusher at the height of his career, though a traumatic and potentially embittering experience, can be a real turning point in his life. Here is how Frank, one such young man, related his experiences to one of our high school drug abuse classes:

"I never intended to get started selling marijuana and dangerous drugs—I don't think anybody does.

"It all started so simply . . . using some joints during my freshman year urged on by the familiar phrase, 'everybody is doing it.' Turning on gave me a pleasant high, so I didn't worry about some of the other things that were happening—like losing interest in sports, and having my grades drop. My English teacher told me I was in danger of flunking, and I replied, 'So what?' and went off to smoke another joint.

"Marijuana can give you a pleasant sensation, but it won't really get you stoned. What it will do is set up an appetite for greater feelings and reactions that can be satisfied only with more powerful and dangerous drugs. And most of the same people who sell grass will carry the other supplies as well.

"Now all of this can get ridiculously expensive—$10 for a lid (ounce of marijuana), about $2.50 for a tab of acid (LSD) or speed. The simplest way to finance your own supply is to go into the business of furnishing. That way your drugs are cheap and you can even make some money on the side. This is exactly what a close buddy of mine and I did—and business was flourishing. It was so good, in fact, I had to convince my folks we had a club which met Friday night (when we made most of our deliveries) in my quarters behind our main house. Carloads of kids were coming and going—so many that one night my buddy had to drive back home and walk the three blocks to my place to bring over more supplies.

"We were really just small high school campus sellers. The older fellows we bought from dealt directly with the underworld syndicate operators who deal in pills and tabs by the thousands and who all too rarely get caught. I've seen thousands of dollars change hands. I've also seen a machine that turns out hundreds of acid tabs in an hour. With these guys, the stakes are big.

"Naturally as our operation got bigger and we got looser, we would sell to anyone, including, as it later turned out, several of the police agents. One day a sheriff's patrol car pulled up in front of my house and it was all over. Both my buddy and I were handcuffed and taken to juvenile hall.

"I frankly figured that I would say what I had to in order to get out, or make the best of whatever time I got, get out, and get back in business—only much more carefully and on a bigger scale. But it didn't work out that way. Bill Neary, my probation officer, has a way of getting to a guy because he really cares, and he knew my blasé front wasn't all that strong. I also met Gordon McLean and the Campus Life staff. What they have to say is simple and straightforward, but it can absolutely get to a guy. They come on with this bit about my whole life being wasted (which it was) . . . I needed to change (true) . . . my life could be different (I doubted it) . . . and that God could make those changes, here, starting now, completely (fantastic!). The last thing I expected would be my life turned in a whole new direction because I accepted the Lord—and in juvie at that. But that is what happened!

"I can say I'm not really wild over the narcs, nor would I ever be one, but press the point and I'll admit being busted was the best thing that ever happened to me. And I shudder to think of what would have happened if I hadn't been stopped when I was.

"So we were different, but that didn't make court any cinch, not with the charges they had on us. My attorney from the Public Defender's Office really had a job on his hands to convince the judge I should be allowed to go home. I was anything but sure I'd make it out of that courtroom free. But we both got that chance, not because we deserved it, but because the judge believed us when we said we'd learned our lesson. I'm sure the judge is told that every day: it was up to us to show him we meant exactly what we said.

"The high school we attend could hardly be expected to welcome back a couple of well-known pushers with bad records, but we are going to school and are thoroughly content to give up our reserved seats in the dean's office to other would-be wise guys.

"Now I'm helping produce the Campus Life "Teen Line" radio show on KLIV, attend the club, and do a lot of speaking to schools like yours, parents' meetings, etc., sharing my experiences. Later on I want to go to college and train for youth work. Maybe I can stop someone else from going down the road I took.

"I'm still a pusher, but I'm pushing something new. It's a great way of living with the Lord . . . and I'm sold on it!"

Since relating these experiences, Frank has spoken to high school students in Brazil on a special assembly tour.

Gary waited for the officer to open the door. Just a second or two was all he needed to make a run for it. The milling crowd of several hundred in the main hall of the teen club would make it easier to ease past any pursuers as he headed for the street where the murky darkness would further aid his escape. Besides, the kids out there all knew him and would do all they could to aid him, of that he was sure.

It had been quite an evening. He had brought some Acapulco Gold to the club and had done a brisk business on the street outside until one of the kids alerted the policeman on duty inside. The officer had responded quickly, managed to collar Gary, and had brought him to a locked office in the back of the club for questioning and to await the arrival of narcotics detectives. The room was well secured, but sooner or later one of the officers would open that locked door, and then, before anyone had time to react, he would be out and gone. He was tense and scared, but this wasn't the first time he had been in a tight scrape.

Problems should have been his middle name. Gary was fourteen at the time, the second oldest of seven children. His father, a construction engineer, was an alcoholic, and the whole family had suffered through the torments of his binges. His father could be nice, too, but he was mean when he drank, and that was more and more of the time.

When you have that kind of problem at home, you can try coping with it, fighting back, or running away. Gary, at various times, had tried all three. He started by trying to live with it and got some good help from Alateen, a program designed to assist youngsters who have alcoholism in their homes. He very much enjoyed the Alateen group discussions and even took part in several presentations the organization made to the public. Alateen helps many young people, but they weren't altogether successful with Gary, maybe because he didn't really let them, or because he had much turmoil inside himself.

At thirteen he was caught breaking into a car, booked into juvenile hall, and released. A few months later, he was picked up for possession and sale of bennies, but again was released to his parents. He lasted one week, then ran away because of the problem with his father.

He hitchhiked to Salt Lake City and got a ride with four men near Provo. They placed him in the middle of the back seat and asked if he had any drugs. When he said, "No," they hit him in the face and one man pulled a knife and made cuts in his side and back (he still has the scars). They finally dumped him out along a deserted section of highway where a passing motorist found him and took him to the county hospital. He found out later from the Utah juvenile authorities that the men who had picked him up had long criminal records: two were heroin users, and two were awaiting trial on manslaughter charges.

He was glad to get back home. Not that he improved any. Far from it. He started to turn on regularly, dropped out of school, and took on all the attitudes and appearances of a regular doper. He turned to furnishing to get money for his own supplies and the teen club was a good place to look for business. . . .

The chance he had been waiting for came. He heard the key turn in the door and the muffled voices of the officers on the other side. Then the door opened.

Gary was up and past the startled officers in a flash, running as hard as he could for the main exit. The uniformed officer blew his whistle and hollered, "Stop that kid!" But the other kids were yelling "Go, Gary, go"—and he did: out the front door, followed by five officers from the Santa Clara Police Department!

He raced around a dark corner into a parking lot where he came to a high fence. He backed up to take a leap at it when an officer grabbed for him. He heard a revolver click and the words, "Halt, or I'll shoot!"

Gary fell down and turned around to look into the faces of four policemen, one of them just releasing the hammer of his gun from firing position.

The court decided Gary needed definite help, so he was committed to the county rehabilitation ranch facilities at Morgan Hill. But no program can help a boy who isn't ready to be helped. He stayed there eight months, made a good adjustment—on the surface at least—and was released.

The third day home he was back on drugs. He

took four reds. "That may be a lot," Gary comments, "but I hadn't had anything for a long time and I wanted them bad."

His life for the next couple of years was a steady series of drug usage and runaways in California and to Phoenix, Arizona. All the time he became more deeply involved, using more, getting better connections, living by his wits when he could and his fists when he had to.

Among the fellows with whom Gary bought and sold drugs was Frank, the young man you met earlier. Frank had a well-earned reputation as a big pusher, and Gary watched Frank go from a respected student downhill to the point where he couldn't think or talk straight for days on end.

"Frank was good at only one thing anymore—selling drugs," Gary said.

Gary himself wasn't far behind. He was out one night with some guys who were hitting heroin, sniffed some stuff, skin popped, and liked it. What he didn't like was what he saw happening to his big-time dope friends. "Those guys shooting heroin were walking death, and I was just about ready to become one of them."

He didn't like the thought of permanent physical and mental damage, but he didn't know how to quit what he was using. And he certainly didn't want to start what they were using, so he seriously contemplated suicide. Instead, he did something entirely out of character for a boy whose whole approach up until that minute had been to run away—he turned himself in to the juvenile authorities!

He didn't know what would happen to him, nor

were the officials really sure what to do with him. So Gary waited a few weeks in juvenile hall while everybody tried to pull the pieces together.

One day at the hall there was a program for the kids, and Gary decided to go to it. It was on drugs and, much to his surprise, Gary knew one of the speakers, Frank.

It was hard for Gary to believe what he saw and heard. Frank was cleaned up, told about getting off drugs, doing well in school and really making something of his future—all the things Gary wanted but believed were beyond his reach. He could hardly wait until the meeting ended to talk personally with Frank. Gary left for his unit at the hall with no doubts in his mind that something had happened to his former drug partner.

He asked the unit officer if he could go in a private room for awhile—another unusual request—because he had some things he just had to think through. He was placed there and spent a long afternoon and evening looking at his life, where he was going, and what had happened to Frank.

The next day he approached Mr. McLean in the juvenile hall corridor, introduced himself, and asked for an interview, which was promptly arranged. Gary told the story you're reading on these pages and then said, "Mr. McLean, if Frank can change, *anybody* can. Frank said yesterday there had been an emptiness and vacuum in his life he had tried to fill with drugs, but now he was on a new high that was much better . . . that never ends . . . and is great. I need it too!"

Gary has made a start on that way of living . . .

through a commitment of faith that can take a boy's frustration and desperation and replace them with a foundation on which he can build a happy, successful life.

A new life is not necessarily built overnight. There can be instability, problems, ups and downs when all a young man has known is insecurity and despair. But Gary has a chance in the California Youth Authority to build on that foundation of commitment a new and better future. Hopefully he will.

He and Frank have been back together again, too. Nothing to worry about, though. Gary has been along as Frank has shared with other teen-agers and adults the facts on a new high—one not found in chemicals.

THE GOD THAT FAILED

Where can the answers be found?

Many students say they try the psychedelic drugs as a mind-expanding experience. They are seeking new values, a sense of purpose and new direction for their lives. If this is the reason many young people use drugs, then the answer to the problem will not be found only in stricter law enforcement, classroom warnings on the evils of drugs, or a variety of other approaches currently being used. Obviously the appeal will have to be made on the basis of how one chooses to live his life. Just to put down drugs will not suffice, for youth will counter by saying our society does not prohibit the use of drugs such as tobacco and alcohol which, in some ways, are more dangerous than many of the hallucinogens or amphetamines.

For these reasons, parents and others who are critical of student drug use must show young people there are better and more lasting ways to experience the fullness, the depth, the variety, and the richness of life than ingesting psychoactive chemi-

111

cals. It is a pity to allow the advocates of LSD to take exclusive possession of the term "consciousness expansion."

But where *can* direction and guidelines be found?

"Many of the traditional avenues to meaning and significance have dried up," points out Dr. Kenneth Keniston, associate professor of psychiatry at the Yale University School of Medicine, in a report given to a national drug abuse conference in Washington. "Traditional religious faith is not, for most sophisticated undergraduates, a means of ascertaining the meaning of life: traditional religions often seem to the students to be worn out, insincere, or superficial. Similarly, the great classic political ideologies, whether they be political liberalism, conservatism, marxism, or fascism, arouse relatively little interest among most undergraduates. Nor does the 'American Way of Life,' as epitomized by 100 percent Americanism and free enterprise, stir most students to enthusiasm, much less provide them with answers about life's ultimate purposes.

"At the same time, many traditional campus activities have lost their centrality as guidelines for or rehearsal of life's ultimate purposes. There was a day when the quest for popularity seemed, to a great many undergraduates, a reflection of a broader philosophy on life in which the most important goal was to make friends, to be popular, and to influence people. Today, the pursuit of popularity and social success is declining in importance, and even those who pursue friendship and social skills most avidly are likely to recognize their limitations as ultimate values. Upward mobility, another ancient American goal, has also lost much of its savor. More and more students arrive in college already 'ahead in the world,' from well-situated middle-class families, and not particularly worried about status and upward mobility. Nor does the old American dream of giving one's children a 'better chance' make great sense to a generation that has been born and bred amid affluence, and that rarely imagines a society in which starvation, unemployment, or depression will be major possibilities.

"One by one, then, many of the traditional sources of meaning have disappeared, at the very same time that academic life itself, because of its intense pressure and professional specialization, seems to many students increasingly irrelevant to their major existential concerns."

One man who faced many of the issues raised here is a friend of the authors, research physicist Lambert C. Dolphin, Jr., of Palo Alto, California. Dolphin described his experiences in these terms to a group of young people at a Campus Life conference:

"Six years of college made me aware of an inner emptiness, sense of inferiority and inadequacy, a feeling of guilt and vague awareness that I was not reaching my full potential as a man. A career in physics and space science proved challenging and financially rewarding but always with a note of disappointment. *There must be more to life than this,* I thought.

"Believing moral standards were relative, I lived experimentally the philosophy, "Eat, drink, and be merry, for tomorrow we die." I wrestled with guilt, becoming more frustrated and discouraged, aware of increasing unhappiness and isolation from others.

"Following the advice of a friend, for two and a half years I invested in psychoanalysis as a means of finding myself, only to discover I was a prisoner of the past, unable to change my basic nature and behavior patterns.

"Sensing deep inner mysteries in the unconscious mind, I became interested in the religions of the world and began to explore and to seek religious experience and spiritual awakening. I came to think that religious truths were relative and quite unable to bring peace of mind.

"With little motivation to live in a meaningless world governed by the laws of chance, I accepted an invitation one day to church. It was there that I discovered the Bible for the first time and became acquainted with the deep, rich insights given by this remarkable document. In a pastor's office not long afterwards, I made the exciting discovery of meeting Christ in a personal experience.

"But gradually during the next few months, I foolishly began to wonder about other religions and how they fit in with the Bible. I was also intrigued at reports of religious experiences resulting from controversial new drugs such as LSD, mescaline, and psilocybin. Troubled by persisting emotional and psychological conflicts. I decided to try the LSD experience with an experimental research group of doctors and psychologists.

"After several preparatory sessions with carbogen gas (which produces momentarily an anesthetic effect), I was ready for my session with a massive dose of LSD and mescaline. A male psychologist and female medical doctor were present in the comfortable living room setting of the research clinic for my all-day trip to LSD-land.

"Shortly after taking the drugs, I began to experience heightened audio and visual perception. Background music became ecstatically alive and full of living richness. The musical instruments became spatially deep and vividly alive inside of me. Vivid color patterns and fantasies in three dimensions filled my mind when I closed my eyes, and with open eyes I perceived the objects in the room with amazing depth, clarity, and a shimmering, crystalline glow. Gradually I lost awareness of my body and seemed to be pulled ever deeper downward into the past and into myself. Strange emotional experiences and long-forgotten dreams bubbled up inside.

"I had the feeling that I was outside myself, looking into thousands of corridors of my life as if I were a whole universe in miniature. At times I seemed to be a vast cathedral. I was aware of history and the past as neither gone nor inaccessible. Time became strangely distorted and I even experienced the terrible sensation of time stoppage and endless eternity.

"Unpleasant and terrible fears associated with conception, birth, and early childhood gripped my mind, and for painfully long periods of time I was caught up in closed cycles of temporary insanity and a terrible vast world of unreality. The environment around me became strangely alive and hauntingly familiar.

"Strange forces and powers seemed to seethe about me, calling and pulling at my soul. And I was aware of the remoteness of God who seemed far off and inaccessible. It did not occur to me to pray. Instead I wondered who I was and how I would ever find myself.

"The immediate effects of the drug wore off that night although until after dark I was aware of the movement and glow of paintings and the animation of photographs which came alive before my eyes.

"The four weeks which followed my LSD session gradually became a living hell. I was aware of a strange, immense spirit world all around me. There were visions of the universe so overwhelming and overpowering I was sure I could never come back to earth. I was obsessed with haunting, seductive voices suggesting suicide or strange behavior.

"While I was aware of people and events, I began to slip out of touch and lose the desire to relate and communicate with my fellow human beings in the everyday world. An overwhelming flood of unconscious material poured through my mind. I was lost in space, unable to sleep for nights on end. Gradually I became aware that something was very wrong, and, gripped by overwhelming fear, I called my pastor. In his office, he drew two circles. One he labelled, 'the material world,' and the other 'the spiritual world.' He showed me that I seemed to be spiritually lost, wandering in a great void between heaven and hell.

"As we prayed together, I gained an immediate sense of the presence of God and a restored relationship of love with Christ. Haunted by terrible visions, I left several days later for two weeks of rest— sleeping, Bible study and long prayer.

"Gradually stability was restored and I began to

relate in real time to real people and to react normally to life on earth. I became aware for the first time of my serious error in taking drugs, my disobedience to God, and the subtlety of temptation.

"Yet six months elapsed before I was fully myself again. Those six months brought the strong and painful discipline of my heavenly Father and inner spiritual surgery which at times was nearly unbearable.

"I had a terrible vision of hell and heard the screams of torment of the lost. I saw that the indirect effects of the drug had brought great inner damage which only time and God could heal. I was so thankful for the steadfast love of God and the miracle of his healing hand.

"Today, fully recovered from the effects of this fantastic experience with drugs and the spirit world, I have been seriously concerned for the growing number of young people who take such drugs. The serious dangers and problems which mind-distorting chemicals present to individuals and to society should be made fully known to everyone."

Mr. Dolphin had men to whom he could go in confidence for help; many community agencies staffed by volunteer professionals and ordinary, concerned people are providing crisis counseling service to young people needing guidance either in person or over the phone. If the youngster lives in Lancaster, Pennsyvania, he can call Teen Problems Anonymous. Hayward, California, has Hope for Youth. In Los Angeles, calls are directed to Hot Line, while Omaha has two centers, Guideline and Personal Crisis Service. In Sacramento, a similar program is called Youth Lifeline. A unique program of help for teens by other teens is D.A.R.E. (Drug Abuse Research and Education) which also conducts seminars for adults and is guided by Dr. J. Thomas Ungerleider of U.C.L.A.

The Teen Line radio program heard on KLIV in San Jose gives a phone number at the end of each program and invites students with personal problems to call anytime during the week. There is a steady stream of response, many of the inquirers involved with drugs. A similar service is offered by Bufe Karraker and Ted Smith who air similar radio programs in Fresno and Stockton, California.

Approaching addiction as primarily a spiritual need, David Wilkerson and his staff have built up a chain of Teen Challenge Centers across the nation to help young addicts. They claim an impressive 80 percent cure rate for those who stay.

As well as the centers, ex-underworld figure Jim Vaus and his Youth Development, Inc. provide an effective service to young people in one of the toughest parts of New York City, Hell Gate Station. On a national level, Young Life, headquartered at Colorado Springs, Colorado, provides a high school club program supplemented by an outstanding summer camping ministry, and makes sure to include young people off the streets of ghetto areas like Harlem. Many of these young people are involved with gangs and drugs. The heartwarming story of this unique work is told in a book well worth reading: *Tough Love* (by Bill Milliken, published by Fleming H. Revell Company).

In California, two men with unique backgrounds

in crime and delinquency head two effective rehabilitation programs which stress a spiritual ministry: Nicky Cruz, a former New York gang leader reached through David Wilkerson's work, leads Outreach for Youth in Fresno; ex-convict Phil Thatcher's Shepherd Foundation in Lynwood works with young offenders as well as prison inmates. Both have written books on their experiences. Cruz's story is told in *Run, Baby, Run,* and Thatcher has written *Under Arrest.*

An interesting study on the drug problem and approaches to it is being made by a group of young men who should know whereof they speak. They are wards of the California Youth Authority in Butte Cottage at O. H. Close School, Stockton. Called D.I.G. (Drug Investigation Group), the program started and is continued by the boys themselves, with the assistance of a sympathetic administration and cottage counselors. Their goal is to evaluate material used in the field of drug education and give good, solid suggestions on how this material can be improved and used more effectively. The boys, all committed for drug offenses, have also gone out from the institution to relate their experiences to audiences in the community and have been very well received. At the heart of the treatment program is the effective use of transactional analysis which helps the young man understand and correct his own attitudes and behavior. At Paso Robles School, another C.Y.A. facility, an extensive student government, policing, and court system has been instituted in Nipomo Cottage as a useful supplement for the counseling program.

Another unique approach to curing addicts is found in the network of Synanon Houses, founded by Chuck Dederich and staffed by ex-addicts who use a program of cold-turkey withdrawal, counseling, and discipline to rehabilitate young addicts. Similar services are provided in many communities by such programs as Pathways, Narcotics Anonymous, the Do It Now Foundation, Odyssey House in New York, and the Seventh Step Foundation, the latter a program designed to help ex-convicts and founded by a San Quentin Prison alumnus, Bill Sands. Sands' rather amazing story is told in two books, *My Shadow Ran Fast* and *The Seventh Step.*

A young black minister in Santa Cruz, California, Eugene Dawson, heads another successful rehabilitation program, Drug Abuse Prevention Centers, with additional centers now in Santa Barbara and Ventura, California, as well as in Aberdeen, Washington. The Narcotic Educational Foundation has been providing helpful programs in the field of drug abuse for many years, and the Salvation Army operates the Manhatten Project in Los Angeles as a referral center for drug users wishing help. "Way Inn," a forty-acre ranch home for boys and girls, is operated by a church near Lancaster, California.

Our own activities in Youth for Christ/Campus Life in the Santa Clara Valley parallel similar programs across the nation, presenting spiritual commitment attractively geared to the non-church crowd in Saturday night programs, and meetings in homes near the schools. Our Drug Abuse Information Service provides educational literature, programs, and counseling for parents and student groups alike.

And that's where Roland first heard of us—when we came to his high school to talk about drugs. Not that he was ready to accept what we said; he wasn't really that impressed, and besides, he had heard it all before. But he was interested in any talk on drugs. An older student who was particularly brilliant had interested him in trying LSD and he had used acid and several other drugs on numerous occasions.

It was a most logical move to start supplying drugs to some of his friends and this Roland did—and was doing when we visited his school. But the school was aware of his activities, as were the police, so it would be only a matter of time until either his own excesses or their investigation caught up with him. When he was finally busted at school, he had just taken a tab of LSD and was hallucinating badly in the dean's office. The police searched him and found twenty-three more tabs of acid, two vials of morphine, and a very interesting little notebook listing various of his customers with the quantity purchased and prices paid for their orders. Roland was taken to the hospital in an ambulance and later was transferred to juvenile hall.

Remembering our school talks, he asked if we would see him at juvenile hall while he was awaiting court hearing, which we did.

Here was a personable, intelligent young man with a great deal of potential—all of it, at that point, negated by his involvement with drugs. He didn't need to be told of the possible effects of acid; he knew more than most teachers. He had read everything available on the subject besides having performed a number of experiments on insects with his supply. In class discussions, he would argue long and eloquently the case for the use of acid as he saw it.

But that last trip had been a bummer. And juvenile hall was not Hilton Hotel, or even like home. Furthermore, the possibility of going to an institution for furnishing was hardly appealing. Most important, the emptiness in his life was still there despite all the drug use. His search for meaning remained unanswered. His problems had gotten greater, not less.

Now, at last, he was ready to listen, and we shared with him how a spiritual commitment to the Lord could fill a void, replace a vacuum, and form the foundation for a whole new life. Some guys might have ignored what we said or snickered behind our backs, but Roland was too disillusioned and frustrated for cynicism.

His commitment was sincere, and we were eager to show the court that the turnabout was far deeper than an emotional reaction to a crisis that could quickly wear off once he was released. Roland was represented in court by our attorney, James Gifford, and was sent home on probation—a real break, to be sure. He is now enrolled in another high school. Roland—like Frank, Pat, and a number of other young people you've met in these pages—helps us regularly in our drug abuse programs for high school students, civic clubs, parents' groups, radio and television. And we repeatedly find that teen-agers will listen to and respect their contemporaries. Besides describing his experiences with LSD and his reaction to court, he often comments on why he took drugs at all:

"LSD for me was a search for love, but the results were only empty and artificial. It was a search for meaning to life, a spiritual high, a looking for God. But He just wasn't to be found there. Please don't give me all the arguments for using drugs; I know those arguments well because I used most of them to cover up what was the real truth—my life was empty, and I thought chemicals could produce a new understanding of God for me. All the drugs did was disillusion and deceive. They made me think I was improving when I was going downhill. They led me to believe my mind was expanding when it was confused and unresponding. They caused me to think I was becoming a more mature person when I was really perpetuating immaturity. Chemicals became my god, and they are the god that failed.

"Chemicals were only the last of many avenues I probed looking for fulfillment in life. But now I've found something that is really great. There's a song about it—let me give you the words:

I looked for love in the red rose so small;
I looked for love in the green trees so tall,
But the red rose had its thorns
And the green tree was a cross . . .
And my searching for love was a total loss.

I looked for love in a friendly face so true;
I looked for love in a creed I once knew;
Well, my friend just called me friend,
And he said, "I'm searching too,"
And the creed only told me what I couldn't do.

And then I heard the story of love like I'd
never known.

How God gave His Son to save me and wanted
    me for His own.
And now I know what it means to belong—
Not lost in a crowd, swept along by the
    throng—
But to Him who gave His life every longing to
    fulfill,
And I know that He loves me, and He always
    will.*

"I can't tell you what to do or how to live your
life. You'll have to decide that. But I do know this
—I'm through with drugs for several reasons, the
most important of which is I've found more lasting
satisfaction in a relationship with the Lord than any
drug ever offered."

To young men and women like this, life has meaning far beyond any chemical vision or temporary
trip. God is the ultimate high. He's a trip that never
ends.

---

* The song "I Looked for Love" was composed by Ralph Car-
michael, copyright 1968 by Lexicon Music, Inc. International
copyright secured. Used by special permission. It is featured on
a record album of the same title from Light Records.

EXPRESSIONS ASSOCIATED WITH DRUGS

Acapulco Gold: High grade of marijuana that comes from Mexico.

Acid: LSD

Acid Head: A regular LSD user.

Backtrack: Withdraw the plunger of a syringe before injecting drugs to make sure needle is in proper place.

Balloon: Rubber toy balloon used for storing or delivering heroin.

Beans
Bennies } Benzedrine.

Bindle: A small paper packet of heroin, morphine, or cocaine.

Black: Opium.

Blast
Blow } To smoke marijuana.

Blow a Stick: To smoke marijuana.

Blue Heaven: Amytal.

Bread: Money.

Brick: Kilo of marijuana in compressed brick form.

Bummer
Bum Trip } A bad LSD experience.

Burn: To accept money and give no narcotic in return, or to give a substance in lieu of.

Burned Out Vein: Collapsed vein.

Busted: To be arrested.

Can: One ounce of marijuana. Term derived from tobacco can in which marijuana was commonly sold in the past. Now more frequently observed in small paper bags.

Cap: A capsule of heroin, commonly a number 5 capsule.
Cartwheels: Amphetamine sulphate tablets, bennies.
Chippy: An occasional user of heroin.
Clean: An addict who is free from narcotic injection marks, or is not in possession of narcotics.
Coasting: Under the influence of drugs.
Cocktail: Attaching a marijuana butt to a regular tobacco cigarette.
Coke: Cocaine.
Cold Turkey: Trying to break the habit. "Kicking it cold turkey" is breaking the habit of drug use without the aid of medication or medical care.
Cook: Underground chemist who manufactures illegal speed, LSD and heroin.
Cop Out: Confess.
Connection: A peddler who knows an addict and will sell him drugs.
Coming Down: Coming off the effects of drugs.
Cottons: Bits of cotton saturated with narcotic solution, used to strain foreign matter when drawing solution up into hypodermic syringe or eyedropper. These cottons often are saved by addicts for an emergency, as they contain a residual amount of the drug.
Crank: Methedrine (or speed).
Crash: Stupor produced by overdose of drugs.
Crutch: Device used to hold marijuana cigarette when it has burned to the point where it will burn the fingers. Also, a container for a hypodermic needle.
Crystals: Methedrine.
Cut: To adulterate narcotics.
Dealer: A drug peddler.
Deck: A small packet of morphine, cocaine, or heroin.
Depressant: Any agent that will depress (decrease) a body function or nerve activity. Depressants may be classified according to the organ or system upon which they act.
Dexies: Dexedrine, Dexamyl.
DMT: Dimethyltryptamine—A short-acting psychedelic drug that is injected or smoked.
Dope: Any narcotic.
Doper: Addict.
Downer: A barbiturate.
Drop a Cap: Swallow an LSD capsule.

Fine Stuff: Drugs of high purity and quality.
Fink: Informer.
Fix, Fix-up: A drug which is about to be injected, or has just been injected.
Flash: To throw up after fixing, or the feeling you get just after fixing.
Frantic: Nervous, jittery drug user.
Freak Out: Bad LSD experience.
Fuzz: The law.
Geeze: Injection of narcotic.
Goof Ball: Any barbiturate tablet or capsule, combined with an amphetamine.
Goofer: One who drops pills.
Goofed Up: Under the influence of barbiturates.
Gram: Gram of heroin (approximately ten capsules).
Grass: Marijuana.
Guide: A person who does not use LSD while sitting with a user during a session.
H: Heroin.
Habit: Addiction to drugs.
Hard Stuff: Morphine, cocaine, heroin.
Hay: Marijuana.
Head: Marijuana user.
Heat: The law.
High: Under the effect of narcotics or drugs.
Hog: An addict who uses all he can get his hands on.
Holding: Possessing narcotics.
Hooked: Addicted.
Horning: Sniffing narcotics up nose.
Hype: An addict.
Horse: Heroin.
Ice Cream Habit: Small irregular habit.
Jamming: Losing one's cool, at a loss for words.
Jive: Marijuana.
Joint: A marijuana cigarette, also prison.
Jolt: An injection of narcotics.
Joy Pop: Inject small amounts of drugs irregularly.
Junk: Heroin, or narcotics in general.
Kee: Kilo (2.2 pounds).
KHIB: Marijuana.
Lid: (See Can).
Loaded: Under the influence of narcotics or drugs.
LSD: Lysergic acid diethylamide tartrate.

Main-liner: One who injects narcotics directly into the veins, intravenously.

Make a Buy: Purchase drugs.

Make it: To buy narcotics. Also to leave.

Man: The law or connection.

Manicure: Prepare marijuana for use in cigarettes.

Mary Jane: Marijuana.

Meth: Methedrine.

Monkey: Drug habit, dependency.

Narcotic (medical): A class of drugs which induce sleep and stupor and relieve pain; includes opiates, anesthetics, and others. Some pharmacologists include barbiturates although they do not relieve pain.

Narc: Narcotics officer or undercover agent.

Nickel Bag: Five dollar purchase of narcotics.

O.D.: Overdose of narcotics—usually heroin.

On a Trip: Under the influence of LSD or other hallucinogens.

Opiate: A class of drugs which have the properties and actions of opium; includes opium itself and derivatives of opium as well as synthetic opiate-like drugs not derived from opium.

Outfit: Equipment for injection by the hypodermic route; a "hype" outfit. Eyedropper, needle, spoon, small piece of cotton, and handkerchief.

Panic: A scarcity of drugs, usually caused by the arrest of a big peddler.

Piece: One ounce of heroin or methedrine.

Pig: (See Hog) Also derogatory term for police officer.

Pill Head: Amphetamine or barbiturate user.

Pop: A subcutaneous injection, usually referred to as "Skin Poppin."

Pot: Marijuana.

Psychedelic: A term invented to describe some of the effects of LSD and similar drugs.

Pusher: Drug peddler to users.

Rainbow
Red Devil } Tuinal.

Red Bird
Red or Reds } Seconal.

Reefer: Marijuana cigarette.

Roach: A partially consumed marijuana cigarette.

Scoring: Making a purchase of narcotics.

Shooting Gallery: A place where heroin addicts congregate to inject their narcotics.

Short: Auto.

Shot: An injection of narcotics.

Source: Where narcotics are obtained: pusher, dealer, supplier, connection.

Smack: Heroin.

Sniffing: Using narcotics by sniffing up the nose, usually cocaine (Snorting).

Snipe: Marijuana cigarette butt.

Snow: Cocaine.

Snowbird: Cocaine user.

Spaced: Very heavily under the influence of drugs.

Speed: Methedrine.

Speedball: A powerful shot of drug, usually heroin or morphine and cocaine combined.

Spike: A hypodermic needle.

Spoon: A quantity of heroin theoretically measured in a teaspoon (usually between one and two grams).

Square: A person who does not know what's happening.

Stash: Place where narcotics or "outfit" is hidden; also, place where a drug peddler will secrete various quantities of narcotics.

Stick: Marijuana cigarette.

Stoned: Under the influence of narcotics or drugs.

Straight Person: A person who is associated with users but does not take drugs.

Strung Out: Addicted (heavily).

Stuff: Heroin.

Taste: A small sample of narcotic.

Tea: Marijuana.

Teenie-Bopper: Youth from upper or middle class who seeks intensified experience from drugs.

Toke Up: To light a marijuana cigarette.

Tolerance: An adaptive state characterized by diminished response to the same quantity of drug or by the fact that a larger dose is required to produce the same degree of pharmaco-dynamic effect.

Tracks: A series of puncture wounds in the veins caused by continuous narcotic injections.

Trip: A psychedelic experience.

Turn On: To use narcotics or to introduce another person to the use of narcotics. To alter awareness (LSD).

Upper: An amphetamine.
User: One who uses narcotics.
Weed: Marijuana.
Weed Head: Marijuana smoker.
Wheels: Auto.
Whites: Amphetamine.
White Stuff: Morphine.
Yellows
Yellow Jacket } Nembutal.
Zig Zag: Paper used to roll marijuana cigarettes.

HELPFUL MATERIALS IN THE DRUG ABUSE FIELD

Here is a list of some of the better materials and sources in the drug abuse field.

Pamphlets

The Crutch That Cripples: Drug Dependence. Department of Medical Health, American Medical Association, 535 N. Dearborn Street, Chicago, Illinois 60610. Available in quantity. Write for prices.

Drug Abuse: The Chemical Cop-Out. National Association of Blue Shield Plans.

Escape to Slavery. Youth for Christ International, Box 419, Wheaton, Illinois 60187. Available in quantity.

Facts You Should Know About Student Drug Abuse, Haskell Bowen and Gordon McLean. Available from D.D. Associates, 717 Loma Verde Avenue, Palo Alto, California 94303.

Parents' Guide to Marijuana. Western Electric Company, Sunnyvale, California 94086.

Books

Blakeslee, Alton, *What You Should Know about Drugs and Narcotics* (New York, The Associated Press, 1969, paperback).

Bloomquist, Dr. Edward, *Marijuana* (Beverly Hills, Glencoe Press, 1968).

Louria, Dr. Donald B., *The Drug Scene* (New York, McGraw-Hill Book Company, 1968).

Wilkerson, David, *The Cross and the Switchblade* (New York, Pyramid Publications, 1963).

Films

Sid Davis Productions, 2429 Ocean Park Boulevard, Santa Monica, California 90405. Recommended is their Youth Guidance film series.

Bailey-Film Associates, 11559 Santa Monica Boulevard, Los Angeles, California 90025. Especially recommended are "The People Next Door" and "Speed Scene."

Family Films, 5823 Santa Monica Boulevard, Hollywood, California 90038. Recommended is "The Youth Drug Scene."

Displays

Narcotics and dangerous drug identification kits and educational charts may be obtained by educational and law enforcement agencies from Winston Products for Education, Box 12219, San Diego, California 92112.

Posters and drug abuse information literature may be obtained by writing: Lamb Enterprises, 1029 Cynthia Avenue, Pasadena, California 91107; K.N.O.W., 262 Orinoco Drive, Brightwaters, New York 11718; Smart Set International, Inc., 1680 N. Vine Street, Hollywood, California 90028.

United States Government materials available include:

Films—Drug Abuse Film Collection, National Audio-visual Center, Washington, D.C. 20409.

Booklets and advertising display cards—Office of Communication, 5454 Wisconsin Avenue, Chevy Chase, Maryland 20015.

Posters—National Institute for Mental Health, Box 1080, Washington, D.C. 20013.

249.1   201)

McLean, Gordon R

High on the campus.

DATE DUE

MAR 7 1971			
AUG 8 1971			
OCT 5 '75			
GAYLORD			PRINTED IN U.S.A.